Praise for *Across the Street and Around the World*

Save two pages for endorsements.

Across the
STREET
and Around the
WORLD

Across the
STREET
and Around the
WORLD

FOLLOWING JESUS TO THE NATIONS IN YOUR
NEIGHBORHOOD . . .AND BEYOND

JEANNIE MARIE

NELSON
BOOKS

An Imprint of Thomas Nelson

Published in Nashville, Tennessee, by Nelson Books, an imprint of Thomas Nelson. Nelson Books and Thomas Nelson are registered trademarks of HarperCollins Christian Publishing, Inc.

Thomas Nelson titles may be purchased in bulk for educational, business, fund-raising, or sales promotional use. For information, please e-mail SpecialMarkets@ThomasNelson.com.

ISBN 978-1-4002-0713-5 (eBook)

Library of Congress Cataloging-in-Publication Data

ISBN 978-1-4002-0742-8

Printed in the United States of America

18 19 20 21 22 LSC 10 9 8 7 6 5 4 3 2 1

For my mom and dad,
You are this book, and I watched you live
out these pages my entire life.
Thank you for loving Jesus, loving people, and loving me.

Contents

CONTENTS

Author Note

I grew up in the Philippine Islands, the daughter of parents with a calling to reach tribal groups with the good news of Jesus Christ. Later, I moved to America to attend a university and, like so many others, ended up working in the corporate world. But as my husband and I started to raise our children, the pull to the nations never hovered far from my soul.

Eventually, I traded in corporate meetings for church staff meetings and threw myself into the world of mobilizing people to pursue God's heart for the nations, working closely with refugees and international students. Along the way God decided to send my family overseas ourselves. Alongside two other families, we moved to a beautiful, hot, humid, chaotic, and colorful Muslim city by the sea in India. There, we established a beachhead for future, long-term, sustainable kingdom work in a city of a million that had, up until then, seen little gospel fruit or influence.

Now, back in America, I am once again advocating for nations without access to Jesus. In my conversations with people like you— people who may have traveled on short overseas trips, been inspired by a speaker to make more of a difference in the world, or who simply enjoy experiencing other cultures—I have found that many are still in need of a simple resource to help them find and live out their global role, and practice reaching out to other cultures step-by-step—right here across the street or around the world.

Because my own global experience has occurred primarily among Muslims, most of the examples I use feature Muslims, but they can relate to other cultural groups as well. You'll discover that the principles and practices we discuss can help you make disciples of anyone—your neighbor, your family, and your coworkers.

For scripture references, I use the New Living Translation, because it gives a fresh perspective without being a paraphrase. Christians can become used to hearing certain verses in a more traditional version and gloss over them without embracing the depth of their meaning.

You might notice that I do not use the traditional word *missionary* in this book, unless I refer to those who traveled overseas with the gospel years ago. This is because the landscape of how nations interact with one another has changed dramatically in the past fifty years, causing an evolution of strategies in foreign missions. I now use the term *field worker* to describe any person who lives cross-culturally, doing a variety of activities, making disciples of Jesus Christ in other nations.

I tell several stories in this book, all of which are true, unless they are told in parable form. These stories are drawn from my own real-life examples or from people I know personally. To protect the privacy and security of the people I write about, however, I've changed the names, locations, and specific details.

As we dive in together, we'll set the stage by discovering God's heart for the nations and how everyone plays a role. We'll look at how to engage the world at our doorsteps—specifically refugees and international students in our communities—and learn how to intentionally cultivate discipleship relationships, so that we're encouraging our cross-cultural friends to follow Jesus Christ. Then we'll learn how to gain global experience, education, and exposure while building a bridge from the nations in our neighborhood to the ends of the earth. Finally, we'll discuss what it would take to surrender the American dream, persevere when things get tough, and hear from God, for those willing to go.

My prayer for you as we go on this journey together is that you will gain confidence, insight, and be able to find your role in reaching the nations. In your life may you have endurance and willingness to "press on to reach the end of the race and receive the heavenly prize for which God, through Christ Jesus, is calling us" (Phil. 3:14) as you develop a heart for all people that mirrors his.

PART ONE

Across the Street

*Following Jesus to
the Nations in Your
Neighborhood*

ONE

Adopting God's Heart for the Nations

Tall, stunning, and dressed head to toe in flowing black, my new Arab Muslim acquaintance strode out the front door of her office to shake my hand.

"It's a pleasure to meet you," she said. "I am Ayisha. Please come inside."

I had never met a Muslim before this moment. I smiled awkwardly, clinging to my two-year-old daughter's hand. I had left the suburbs and driven into the city on a personal quest: to practice global compassion in my local context. I swallowed hard and dragged myself into the modest refugee resettlement office.

Ayisha sat me down, poured me coffee, and wasted no time. "Why are you here?" she asked evenly.

I stumbled across the thoughts jumbling around in my head, trying to think how to explain. I decided on genuineness.

"I'm a follower of Jesus, whom you call *Isa al Masih,* and I'm trying to put his words into practice."

I glanced around the bare office, which overlooked squares of government housing. Countless Sudanese made their homes in those blocks, only an hour from my white-picket-fenced backyard.

3

"I know this might sound kind of crazy, but I was reading his teaching about loving your enemy," I continued.

Ayisha's black hijab hugged her neck and forehead, framing her luminous, beautiful eyes and porcelain face. I wondered what had brought this educated, poised woman to America.

She leaned forward, and the gesture encouraged me to continue.

"Jesus says to love your enemies and pray for those who do harm to you. I can't think of any enemies, except people I don't really know. Because of 9/11, the thought crossed my mind that countries and people from different world religions often *perceive* each other as enemies. So maybe I should do something about that by actually getting to know a Muslim."

I pulled my daughter up on my lap and squeezed her tight. I wasn't sure how Ayisha would respond.

She didn't say anything, so I continued, "Well, then Jesus tells a story about the Son of Man coming on the clouds of heaven to judge the world. All the nations of the world stand before him, and he separates the sheep from the goats. To the sheep he says, 'Come and share in my master's happiness. I give you the kingdom that I've prepared for you since the beginning of time.' His reason for giving them the kingdom? He says that when he was hungry, someone fed him. When someone was thirsty, they gave him water to drink. When someone was sick or in prison, a person visited him. When someone was a stranger, or a foreigner, a person welcomed him. Whenever they did this to someone who needed it, it was like they did it for Jesus."[1]

I paused, and still she said nothing. I took a deep breath.

"Someone told me that Iraqi refugees were coming to Phoenix. So I looked it up online and found your name. It sounded Muslim. I thought it would be good for me to actually meet a Muslim. You also said on the phone that you're helping refugees, so I thought, well, maybe I could help somehow."

"Yes," she finally said, "you can help."

I breathed a sigh of relief and smiled to myself. I envisioned organizing a food drive or a clothes-collection campaign. I pictured all the refugees gathering around, hugging my friends and me in gratitude. We would all smile at each other and then go home.

Instead, Ayisha said, "I just met a young widow with three small children, who arrived last month from Iraq as a refugee. If all that you are saying is true, then I would like you to come with me to her apartment tomorrow." She paused before continuing. "American soldiers accidentally killed her husband. I would like you to come with me and ask forgiveness for the American people."

Stunned at her request, I heard myself whisper meekly, "Yes, I will go with you." My heart quaked with equal parts anticipation and angst as I felt deeply both my smallness and God's greatness.

After all, I hadn't always been the kind of person to trek across the city in search of random Muslims to befriend and refugees to help. God had to reveal his heart for the nations to me first.

Awakening to God's Heart for the Nations

My path to falling captive to God's heart for the nations was long and winding. I, like many others, held misconceptions about my involvement in cross-cultural relationships. But that's exactly what they were: misconceptions. So much of the time, we think getting involved with people from other countries or faith backgrounds is too complicated, so we leave it for someone else to do. But this may actually be keeping us from discovering a deep, integral part of God's character, purpose, and will—and the part he asks us all of us to play in expanding his kingdom. Rather than miss out on the adventure it is to follow Jesus to the nations, let's take a closer look at some of the things many of us say to ourselves that keep us from joining in.

"It's Not My Thing."

Sometimes, we notice people involved in missions or global causes and think of it as a hobby, sort of like someone who might be an avid fisherman, a quilter, or a skydiver. We hear a story like my encounter with Ayisha, and we say, "Good for them. But that's not my hobby." Or we might take it up a notch and view those missional people who would try to help refugees, for example, as called to a worthy cause, in the same vein as those who advocate for natural health remedies, prayer in schools, or homeschooling. We say, "Good for them. But my cause is different from theirs."

I grew up as the child of expats living overseas, privy to firsthand stories of tribal groups without access to the gospel. I even lived in a tribe as a child and still I thought, *This is my parents' thing, not mine.* But one day, God opened my eyes, and I saw his plan for all nations to worship him—starting in Genesis and ending in Revelation—and that he meant for *all of us* to be involved in it. Could it be that crossing cultures, being a light to the nations, wasn't a hobby or a cause relegated to a few, but a purpose in which everyone could play a role because God planned it that way from the beginning?

God told Abraham, "I will bless you and . . . *all the families on earth will be blessed through you*" (Gen. 12:2–3, italics mine). Throughout the Old Testament, God kept pressing Israel to be a light to the world, sending Jonah to the Ninevites, Daniel to the Babylonians, and Esther to the Persians. He placed Jerusalem "at the center of the nations," with lands around her, so the people called to stay at home could still affect the surrounding nations (Ezek. 5:5). God told the prophet Isaiah, "I will make you a light to the Gentiles, and you will bring my salvation to the ends of the earth" (Isa. 49:6).

The apostle Peter brought Abraham's "blessed to be a blessing to the nations" covenant right into the New Testament too. He reminded everyone that we are all descendants of Abraham and that "through your descendants all the families on earth will be blessed" (Acts 3:25). So that means us too. God blessed you and me with the good news, so that all the nations on the earth—all the families of the earth—will be blessed with the good news through us.

The thread weaves right through to Revelation, where we catch a vision for the result of God's heart for the nations. The apostle John saw the future, with heavenly creatures encircling the throne of God, saying to the Lamb, who is Jesus Christ, "You are worthy to take the scroll and break its seals and open it. For . . . your blood has ransomed people for God from every tribe and language and people and nation" (Rev. 5:9). People from *every* tribe, *every* language, and *every* nation will one day stand shoulder to shoulder next to you and me in front of the throne of God! This means that reaching out to every culture isn't just a few people's "thing." It is God's "thing." The closer we come to experiencing God's heart to see people from all nations reconciled back to him, the more our eyes will open to his heart for the whole world.

Like a blind person who could suddenly see, I too could see—through God's eyes. The scales fell off, and I saw the millions and millions of people around the world, some of them moving in across the street, without even the opportunity to know God. I felt restless, wrestling with conviction, about this ultimate injustice

REACHING OUT TO EVERY CULTURE ISN'T JUST A FEW PEOPLE'S "THING." IT IS GOD'S "THING."

and wondered about my role in it. I wanted to *do* something about it. But then I fell victim to the next common misconception.

"I don't see myself moving overseas right now, so there's not much I can do."

Sometimes we believe that if we're not ready to move to a jungle somewhere in Papua New Guinea, or since we're not physicians educated to eradicate diseases in Africa, there's just not much else we can do to be involved around the world.

I spent eight years after university just living life, going to church, working, raising children, scrapbooking, playing volleyball, and planning vacations. Not a bad life, but a life without much spiritual excitement. I had absolved myself from any responsibility or privilege to be a light to the nations, and even our own community, because my husband and I didn't see ourselves living in a tribe somewhere.

Then 9/11 happened. Suddenly the rest of the world came crashing in on my everyday life. The news, the issues the rest of the world faced, the *nations*—all of it started affecting my little, private, safe bubble, whether I wanted it to or not. I couldn't isolate myself anymore from the issues of an increasingly interconnected world. But what could I do to be a light—like Israel to the nations—from my house in the suburbs of America?

Then, a friend of my father's landed on our doorstep one day for a visit. He was from India and brought with him a charismatic personality and a fresh faith in God for miracles. My somewhat uneventful and ordinary life came alive with spiritual possibility and adventure as I listened to him and caught his vision for championing the cause of orphans and widows from a country that housed one-third of the world's poor and only a tiny fraction of the population following Jesus. We talked about the possibilities of speaking, writing, praying, raising funds, and even leading short trips. I hadn't realized how much I could do right where I lived to make an impact on people on the other side of the world.

Then, as opportunities opened up to advocate for the nations, my experiences gradually deepened. God encouraged me to make disciples right where I lived, befriending refugees and international students who were already in my city—and that's when I found myself having dinner with Ayisha and the young widow from Iraq. One summer, I found myself in the Sahara desert, sitting in the tents of refugees without a country, and listening to imams (Muslim spiritual leaders) and pastors debate about our ancestor Abraham. Another time I ended up in a little hut-turned-church on the top of a mountain in the Philippines, hearing tribal believers, former animistic spirit worshippers, tell riveting stories about my parents, who had lived and worked in their tribe thirty years before. And then, as sometimes happens, God eventually led my husband, our children, and me to India, to live and work in a city where few Westerners had made their homes.

God's global heart within all of us could burst forth in many forms. We might be called to stay—as visionary mobilizers, extravagant givers, passionate people of prayer, or effective administrators undergirding those who go. Or, God's global heart might thrust us into effective welcoming roles, launching us into communities of refugees or into universities to befriend international students. As we practice following Jesus by discipling the nations in our neighborhoods, he may even lead us to eventually exchange one continent for another as we remain open to his leading. We discover our role in reaching the nations, though, by starting small, and starting soon, by making friends with people from other countries.

Personalizing God's Heart for the Nations: Make a Friend

We may find our hearts stirring for the nations, and even embrace the idea that we could make a global difference right where we already live, but then get stuck because we don't know how to get started. Here's one fun and life-changing suggestion: make an international friend! Putting a face that's a friend to the big word *nations* helps us fall in love with God's heart for all cultures. We'll discuss how to welcome refugees and international students in chapter 3, but before then, here are a few suggestions on how to find friends from another country who live right where you live.

First, eat at ethnic restaurants. My friends and I look for small, family-run ethnic restaurants—Arabic, Turkish, Vietnamese, Thai, Indian, Filipino, Lebanese, the choices are endless. We try to meet the owners, ask for their recommended dishes, and order generously. Our tables often get filled with samples and desserts on the house because we show genuine interest in learning about their countries, their food, and their lives. My husband and I once met a Pakistani husband with an Indian wife who ran a small restaurant called Currys and Kabobs. We gained a great deal of insight from them about arranged marriages, the political climate in the two countries, and their views on Christianity, Hinduism, and the sects of Islam found there. All because we took the time to go out for dinner and start a conversation.

Another thing we can do is adjust our leisure activities, like working out at the gym or playing basketball in a community league, electing to do them in areas of our cities where internationals are likely to live. With young children in tow, my mom friends and I planned playdates with each other at parks around our city where the engineers and software developers from India tended to live, or near the apartment complexes where refugees resettled, or near the block where international students rented out apartments next to our state university. We'd make friends through our children and have leisurely conversations about family and life. One of these park playdates turned into a regular playdate each week with a group of Muslim moms who also took their kids to play at a particular park, which then turned into visits to each other's houses. Eventually, my friend and one of her new friends started an interfaith discussion group designed to seek God together. The group drew as many as twenty women at a time from both Islam and Christianity to discuss how to follow God together.

Another idea for finding friends from other cultures is to intentionally notice and approach people who are already part of our everyday lives, at work, school, or play. For example, I noticed an Asian woman with a strong accent at my son's community soccer team practices. I sat next to her one afternoon and simply asked, "What country is your family originally from?" This question is less offensive than one that assumes they recently came from another country. People from other cultures living in our Western cities are often citizens, so it's best not to assume otherwise. However, their cultural ties to their families' countries of origin are often strong and fresh. This particular soccer mom had moved to America from China to birth her second child, since, at that time, the Chinese government only allowed one child per family. During those soccer practices, I learned more about her family, her culture, and the way her atheist beliefs mixed with ancestor worship. After one of our soccer games, she took me to what she called "the most authentic Chinese restaurant in town," and I tried cold duck and salt seaweed for the first time.

We can also take advantage of any opportunity that presents itself—or that God arranges when we pray for it. My husband and I bought a used car from an ad on the internet one time and, by chance, we bought it from an international student. As we exchanged the keys and a check, I asked, "Have you ever been in an American home before? Why don't you come over for dinner sometime?" The student came the next weekend, brought friends, and stayed until midnight, playing songs on our guitar with our children singing along, showing our whole family photos of his country, and even calling his family back home to say hello to us.

After we get some experience realizing how receptive people from other cultures are to conversations with a stranger, we can try approaching people we see on the street, in the grocery store, or anywhere, and say hello to them. When I see a woman wearing a head covering or a hijab, I know that she's used to getting stares, frowns, or being ignored, as if she's invisible. A simple greeting in Arabic, *"Assalamualaikum"* (Ah-sah-lah-mu-ah-lay-coom), usually starts a lively conversation with lots of smiles and welcome. Once, at church, a woman dressed in a traditional Indian sari showed up with her family. My husband and I greeted them with hands folded to our chests in a prayer style and, with bows and smiles, said, "Hello! *Namaste!*" They brightened, and we talked about our mutual interest in India. We ended up at their house for dinner that night, meeting all their extended family at a birthday party they happened to be hosting. It's good to get educated on universal greetings and use them in obvious situations. People always appreciate that you're trying to create bridges and show interest in them.

Using waiting time intentionally—at doctors' offices, the DMV, or the airport—also gives us opportunities to scan the crowd for an international person to sit beside. On a four-hour layover, my husband and I entered the Southwest gate waiting area. He noticed the elderly Indian grandmother in a sari with an empty seat beside her first and ushered me over. I sat next to her, smiled, and said, "Where are you going?" She didn't stop talking until we boarded, telling us all about her family and basically her whole life, and then she saved a middle seat next to her for me on the plane. I disembarked with a new recipe for vegetable curry from Punjab and sweet kisses on my cheek for her new "adopted daughter." She left with a paper full of drawings illustrating the hope that Jesus gave of freedom from the endless cycle of reincarnation that she both feared and accepted as inevitable.

Another idea is to use commuting time intentionally. When we take public transportation, like the bus or light rail, often we find refugees on a budget, or international students without a car in the country, to sit beside. I know a pastor that takes Uber every chance he gets, even just to attend a meeting across town, because a lot of Uber drivers come from other countries and use Uber to supplement their income. On my most recent Uber experience, my husband and I met a gentleman originally from Ghana who was a Christian and quick to share *his* faith with us. As we pulled up to our destination, my husband prayed a blessing over his business and his family, and for God to intervene in a difficult situation he had shared about his son.

Lastly, we can hang out with people we know who themselves hang out with people from other cultures. I asked one friend who seemed to know a lot of people from other countries if I could tag along next time he met with someone. The next evening, he invited me to go to a potluck at the Hare Krishna temple with him and his family and their Hare Krishna friend from Kolkota, India. "What?!" I said. "Can we *do* that?" Turns out we can! They welcomed us, fed us lots of curried rice and vegetables and, with all the orange robes and shaved heads, I felt as if I had walked into a different era, in a different country.

You should know that I'm not any different than you are. I'm just a regular, ordinary person who still takes a deep breath and says a quick prayer before approaching a stranger from another country, just as you would. Basically, though, I'm willing to make myself available and be intentional. If we stay in tune with God's Spirit leading us and try to notice opportunities, taking a small step toward those opportunities to see what will happen, God will put our willingness, our friendliness, and our openness to good use, for his purposes in drawing all people from every nation to him.

The Essential Ingredient: Follow Jesus

Once we try some of the ideas I just shared to make a friend, we may wonder how to go about making an actual difference in their life, and how to know what to say or do that reflects the light we're supposed to shine to the nations. The simple answer is, follow Jesus. At the end of the day, who we are in Christ is more important than what we say, or what we do, or even where we live. If we connect with Jesus daily, spending time in God's Word, praying to and worshiping God regularly, then his Spirit will inform us and guide us. As we make ourselves available, he will tell us what to say, where to go, and what to do, when it's the right time to say it, go somewhere, or do something.

AT THE END OF THE DAY, WHO WE ARE IN CHRIST IS MORE IMPORTANT THAN WHAT WE SAY, OR WHAT WE DO, OR EVEN WHERE WE LIVE.

I felt this utter dependence on God's Spirit to guide me as I followed Jesus—and Ayisha—to visit Hajer, the young widow from Iraq. As we entered the one-bedroom apartment, Hajer smiled a welcome, holding a little girl on her hip, with two other children peeking out from behind a chair. She offered me a spread of biryani chicken simmered in spices; tabbouleh, a chopped salad with a sharp vinaigrette taste; and baked bread. Even with the little she had, her desire to be hospitable and honor a guest meant she served her best. After we ate I took Hajer's hands in mine. Looking into her eyes, with tears, I said, "I grieve with you about your husband. It should not have happened. And now you are here, in this strange country. I want to tell you that I'm glad you have come to my country. And I want to ask forgiveness for the American people."

Initially, she murmured, "It's okay. No, no, don't worry."

"No. It's not okay," I urged. "Your husband should not be gone, and you should not be here, alone in this new country."

All three of us women then cried together, recognizing her great loss.

"Hajer," I said, "I was praying for you last night, and I believe God gave me a story that he wants you to hear."

She nodded to listen.

"Your name is the very first time in the *Torah* [Arabic for the Old Testament] that an angel of the Lord calls a woman by name."

She knew part of the story, because it appeared in her holy book also. (*Hajer* is Arabic for Hagar.)

"Perhaps you feel like the Hajer in the *Torah*, crawling in the desert, cast out from her community, desperate with sadness, and feeling like she wants to die. Right now, you probably feel as if God can't see or hear you and, like her, you're ready to give up and you wonder how you, alone in a strange country, will provide for your three children."

Her tears confirmed that she indeed felt this way.

"But then the angel of the Lord appeared to Hajer!" I announced.

"And what did he say?" Ayisha demanded.

It was an unlikely scenario, the first Muslim woman I had ever met, eagerly listening to a Bible story and translating it for another Muslim woman. At that moment, I also understood why Jesus told stories to people so often.

"The angel of the Lord told her that he would take care of her and would bless her son. Hajer felt known and seen. So she called him 'You are the God who sees me,' and the water well there was even named 'well of the Living One who sees me' [Gen. 16:7–14]. Hajer, God sees you right now. He will take care of you as you look to him.

He will take care of your children, and he will give you what you need to provide for them."

She nodded, tears slipping down her cheeks, one hand still clutching mine. We prayed together, our open eyes looking to the ceiling. She released my hand to hold her palms face up to receive this comfort from God for her and her children, a common gesture for Muslims when they pray. She then brought her hands to her face to receive the blessing brought by the story.

In any interaction with people from other cultures—really, with anyone at all—Jesus is our model for knowing what to say and what to do. That day, Hajer received a taste of what Jesus said he came for: "The Spirit of the LORD is upon me, for he has anointed me to bring Good News to the poor. He has sent me to proclaim that captives will be released, that the blind will see, that the oppressed will be set free." (Luke 4:18–19). Jesus walked into places of brokenness, lostness, and darkness—places where he found people craving wholeness, love, and light. Today, just as it was during New Testament times, people like Ayisha and Hajer often have little access to Jesus' message and little access to Jesus' people. This is true both of places around the world and right in our own backyard.

As we interact with soccer moms from China, Uber drivers from Ghana, and elderly grandmothers from Punjab, let's speak life over people by demonstrating the way life is supposed to be, as Jesus did. Because of our close connection with Jesus, ours should naturally be the life that pours expensive perfume on Jesus' feet in a humble act of genuine worship, to the whispers of disapproval about this choice (John 12:3–5). It's the life that turns over the tables of money changers in the Lord's temple, speaking of justice in God's house, in an act of righteous rage because "passion for God's house will consume me!" (John 2:13–17). It's the life that fills jars of oil for starving widows while hiding from authorities who wish you dead, and speaks life and faith into action (1 Kings 17:8–16). It's the life that spends all night praying on a mountain and then chooses twelve disciples to follow him (Luke 6:12–16). Lavish worship, zeal for justice, extreme faith, intense communication with God—all four of these stories illustrate how Jesus modeled the life we are called to live.

As we walk in the footsteps of Jesus right where we live, work, and play, fully alive to God's heart for the nations, with confidence we can make ourselves available to friendships from people in other cultures. Let's spend a few minutes asking God to help us see the world as he sees it, for our hearts to mirror his heart, and for new friendships as we follow Jesus:

God, please shatter any misconceptions I have about my role in reaching the nations. I want to believe that from the very beginning you meant to bless me with the good news of Jesus so that I could be a light that would bless the whole world. I commit to starting somewhere, starting small, and starting soon by making a friend. Fill me with your Spirit, Jesus, and let me always walk in step with you so that my words, my actions, and my character reflect you to my new friends.

Reflection

1. How do the desires of your heart—and the actions of your life—match God's desire for people from every nation to worship him?
2. Which ideas could you try this week to meet people from other countries living right where you live?
3. What do you need to do to foster a deeper relationship with Jesus in your personal life so that your character, actions, and words reflect his?

TWO

Interacting with Other Cultures Well

When Joel and Hannah, friends of mine, started trying to meet people from other countries, I invited them to join a missional group whose members spurred each other on to be more intentional with their friendships. One Sunday night they pulled up to the bustling apartment complex on the outskirts of Phoenix, where the group met. They glanced at their toddler, Oliver, sleeping peacefully in his car seat. Feeling unsure about this inner-city location, Joel locked the van door before they headed toward the building.

When they walked into the apartment, they stepped over a pile of shoes where everyone had left them and entered barefoot. Several blond-haired kids ran under their legs and out the door, chasing one another.

Joel and Hannah squeezed by some young adults sitting on the floor, the couch, and the counter, filling up every available space. Joel tentatively asked someone nearby, "Hey, is this the group where we learn to reach out to people in other cultures? Sorry, we came a little early."

"Oh, no worries. Yes, this is it. Welcome, and sorry about the chaos! Some of us just got back from hanging out with a group of international students. We're excited about debriefing it. The folks with families are trying to get their kids fed first."

Another woman overheard them and, seeing the sleeping Oliver, said, "Let me show you the room where all the kids get put down to sleep later tonight while we talk." She walked Hannah into one of the back bedrooms, where a row of towels lined the floor as makeshift beds.

Hannah gulped. She thought of Oliver's bedtime routine that she performed at exactly the same time each evening in a quiet room with a safe crib. "How do you keep them from crawling away?" she asked, raising her eyebrows.

"Oh, they learn! The other kids will watch out for your little one too. Pretty soon he'll be able to sleep anywhere!"

Hannah hesitated, but eventually laid her son down on a nearby towel and followed the woman back to the living room, where everyone sat cross-legged on the floor around a few large communal platters heaped with Moroccan stew. She settled next to Joel and took a cue from the rest of the group, as they scooped rice with their hands and laughed at the mess they made. Once the meal wound down and the children snuggled into various laps and corners of the apartment, the leader, sitting on a low stool, started to talk.

"All right, who met with someone new this week? How did you respect their culture? Who did you pray with? Anyone invite someone to study the Bible with them?"

The people in the group told stories of their spiritual conversations and discussed new observations and learnings. They described practical ways they had loved their friends that week, some of the cultural cues they noticed, and how they had observed some friends move toward the kingdom of God.

"That's cool how God answered your friend Bassui when you prayed with him," said the leader to a single guy who led a hiking group. To another young woman he said, "And how you spent the day learning to cook with Fatima. Next week you're on for dinner for everyone! Love that you discussed the story of the woman at the well and that she wants to hear more."

After a few more stories, the leader led the group into prayer. Over the next hour, they asked God to intervene, prayed for spiritual awakening, and listened to the Holy Spirit for next steps with their friends. Periodically someone would start singing a song or reading a verse. All the while, mothers nursed and parents quietly stole away to shush their children to sleep.

Toward the end of the evening, the leader asked Joel and Hannah to share what had motivated them to join this missional group.

"Wow. I'm not sure how we're going to do this, actually," started Hannah. "Recently, we took a two-week trip overseas. It opened our eyes to the need to reach out to people from other cultures, and we wanted to learn how to do that. Maybe prepare ourselves for something God might have for us in the future." She hesitated. "But this is a bit intense. How will we find all this time to spend with people like you guys do? And what if we offend them? We don't even know their culture yet."

Joel looked a little nervous too. "We really want to do this, but spending a couple hours a week with people from other countries, a couple hours praying, and then this group night once a week? I don't know how you have the time to do all this. I mean, I work, and I know you all work too. Some of you are studying full-time . . ." He trailed off and noticed the nodding heads and understanding glances.

"We'll help you," reassured the leader. "The fact is that joining a group to practice all this together means we all actually do it. You just have to be willing to try a few new things and rearrange the priorities in your life."[1]

Recognizing That We Really Are Different

Maybe you feel like Joel and Hannah: ready to make a friend from another country, to put your growing interest in the nations into practice right where you live, but unsure about how you'll come across to someone from another country. You're probably right to feel this way, and that's a good posture from which to learn. Americans, in particular, lack experience setting foot in foreign countries, unlike people from other Western cultures. Only one-third of Americans own a passport. And with a country bordered by two oceans, and thousands of miles to travel within itself, the majority of Americans spend their entire lives without crossing an international border. This inexperience often leads to certain perceptions and assumptions about other cultures, the first one being that we're not that different.

As Craig Storti, in *Americans at Work: A Guide to the Can-Do People*, explained, "While Americans accept that people from other cultures may be foreign on the surface, Americans believe that 'underneath we're all alike.' They believe that any differences that do exist between themselves and non-Americans are ultimately insignificant."[2]

Basically, we assume that the underlying motivations, reasoning, and values we have are the same as those anyone else has. And while someone may speak another language or enjoy different foods, we all come from the same fundamental understanding and place. But when we come to know different cultures, we see that this is simply not true.

If Joel and Hannah can realize that Westerners view and manage relationships, communication, decisions, time, resources, and hospitality much differently than those from Eastern countries, it will give them a head start in interacting with them. In general, Western cultures value and emphasize individuality, efficiency, task achievement, individual decision-making, personal space, and instant access to goods and entertainment. These often directly contrast with Eastern cultural values, which emphasize communities, adaptability, flexible timing, relational achievement, and group decision-making. As we interact with Eastern peoples, we might also notice they have little concept of personal space, and most must work and wait for pleasure-based activities and belongings.[3]

So, as we seek to step into cross-cultural relationships, it's helpful to first identify what high-level "brand" of culture our new friends come from, in what general ways it might differ from our own, and then learn to adjust our expectations and actions accordingly.

Laying Down Our Preferences

Now that we realize cultures have specific preferences in major areas of life, and they'll likely clash with ours, we have some personal heart issues to examine. How willing are we to lay down our own cultural preferences to honor those of another? Even if they live in our own country?

Paul the apostle wrote, "When I was with the Jews, I lived like a Jew to bring the Jews to Christ. . . . When I am with the Gentiles who do not follow the Jewish law, I too live apart from that law so I can bring them to Christ. . . . Yes, I try to find common ground with everyone, doing everything I can to save some" (1 Cor. 9:20–22).

As Westerners, we like to do things the way we prefer to do them. We like to wear what we want to wear and to eat what we feel like eating, when and how we want to eat it. It doesn't generally occur to Westerners to try to match someone else's cultural preferences, because we value individual style, encourage unique opinions, and teach tolerance for individual preferences in our schools. But laying down the way we do things, giving up what we like to eat or wear, to try to identify with someone else serves and values the other person. When we enter into their world, surrendering our cultural preferences, we do what Jesus did when he entered our world. He became human so he could identify with us in every way. He laid down his privileges, his wealth, his power, and his rights so that we could accept him and hear his message. We could experience his message firsthand, because he became one of us (Philippians 2).

Even if we are willing—or become more willing—to lay down our cultural preferences in service to others, sometimes there are simple things we just don't know. When it comes to culture, there are so many potential pitfalls, and we could easily offend someone and be completely unaware. For example, if we eat with our left hand in most non-Western cultures, it means we're eating with the hand that's used to clean oneself after using the bathroom, in lieu of toilet paper. Or, if we have a dog as a pet and invite Muslim friends over, we might not know that after touching a dog, they're required to fully wash themselves seven times, since dogs are considered unclean. Hundreds of other taboos like this will catapult us into numerous cultural blunders, even with the best intentions. We can't possibly get everything right. So what are we to do?

Here are four tips for entering into a new cultural situation with a little savvy that will go a long way.[4]

Tip #1: Be a dummy.

Everyone likes to feel smarter than another person. Play the humble role, admitting that you don't know what's appropriate to wear, or eat, or say—or any number of things—and you'll have a much better chance of being accepted. When you admit that you're foreign to the culture and don't have a clue, which is the truth, you lower the bar of expectation and prepare others for your potentially inappropriate behavior. It also gives the people in the other culture a chance to teach you what's appropriate. When you do something you shouldn't be doing, instead of judging you, they'll laugh and correct you, knowing you need their help. The key, of course, is to remember and do what they say, so you don't lose respect and can keep growing in your cultural awareness.

Tip #2: Ask how they would do it.

"Can I wear underwear on my head?" you ask.

"Yes! Yes, of course you can," most people in another culture will say if you ask such a direct question. So as not to offend, they will likely say yes to *any* question you ask. Since honoring guests is such a high value, they will bend over backward to let you do whatever they perceive you want to do. It would be impolite to say no. A better way to ask such a question is to use a third-party illustration.

"If your daughter were here with us now, would you allow her to wear underwear on her head?"

Then they would laugh and say, "Of course not. No one wears underwear on their head *here*."

If you are an astute listener and caught the word "here" tacked on to the end of the sentence, you might probe a little more: "If not here, then *where* would your daughter wear underwear on her head?"

"Well, of course if she attends the muckawuka dance event, then she *must* wear underwear on her head!"

Fictional muckawuka dances and underwear aside, the principle from this humorous illustration applies to real-life situations more than you know. Let's not corner our host with a "can I" question. Give your cross-cultural friends the freedom to answer what they know we need to know by starting with "Would *you* . . ."

Tip #3: Don't be the first, and don't be the last.

If you're not the first person to start eating, then you can watch the first person and do what they do, how they do it, right after they do it. Watch how they pick up their fork—or, in many cases, how they scoop the rice with their hand. You can watch how they signal that they're finished before your plate gets filled to the brim . . . again! If you're not the last person done eating, then you can let that last person do whatever is traditionally done in that culture. Perhaps the last person done eating is supposed to get up and leave, or offer the traditional tea. Who knows? You'll know, if you're not the last person to finish.

Tip #4: If not sin, do it their way.

So that you don't draw unwanted—or unintended—negative attention to yourself, it's wise to try to do everything the way your cross-cultural friends do it, if it's not sin. The fact is, sometimes we don't know why things are done a certain way, and it might mean something important in that culture. Most people do things a certain way. And they've been doing it that way for a long time. Sometimes the way they do it means something, and sometimes it doesn't. But we'll never know until we've been immersed in the culture awhile.

For example, is it so bad that you like to wear red when everyone else in the community you're visiting wears brown all the time? It could be. Until you know why they wear brown all the time—and even sometimes when you *do* know why—it's a good idea to just wear brown too. Do it their way.

What about if they're in your country? Is it so bad to wear what you're used to wearing on a hot summer Saturday, shorts and a tank top, when you visit friends from a different culture? After all, they're in your country, you might think. But if all the women in that culture wear clothes that fully cover their arms and legs and that hang loosely around their waists, let's dress in their version of modesty too.

Other times the line between cultural preference and moral ethics blurs. In that case, Peter and the other apostles said to obey God, rather than human beings (Acts 5:29). For example, on a short-term trip, is it so bad to offer a bribe to a police officer who pulls you over, when he asks you to say you don't really have nine people stuffed in your five-seater car in exchange for a few hundred rupees, just as you've seen the locals do? Yes. It is. In this case, since lying is a sin, don't do it their way.

Six Critical Habits for Entering Other Cultures Well

If we're living in a Western country and haven't spent a lot of time around various cultures, we may need a little more help adjusting our overall ways of living to project a feeling of welcome to people from cultures different from our own. The likelihood that our current living habits will allow us the opportunity to interact well with those from Eastern cultures—and thus blocks of people farthest from Jesus, like Hindus, Muslims, and Buddhists—is small. But if we can develop a few new habits, our lives can realign to do just that. We will need to practice new ways of *living*—and new ways of *being*.

It's like preparing to run a marathon. Once you've made the decision, you'll start to form new habits that become part of your everyday life until you can eventually run twenty-six miles in a row. In the same way, if we wish to make crossing cultures a significant part of our lives, we will need to create new habits. And these habits will actually help us rearrange our lives in such a way that we'll be able to reach out to *any* nonbelievers living around us, not just those from other cultures.

These habits will take practice, and they will take time! But you can ease into it by trying one habit this month and adding another habit the next month until your lifestyle has shifted to accommodate relationships with nonbelievers, and those from non-Western cultures. You'll be surprised at the new normal you'll start to live.

Habit #1: Be intentional about where you invest your time and energy.

When someone asks us to join a club, go to an event, or start up an initiative, we can ask ourselves, "Does this give me more relationships with nonbelievers or people from other cultures?" We will need to say no to very good things in order to say yes to the very best things, based on the focus God gives us at the time. To give more time to people in other cultures, we'll need to constantly reevaluate and realign our priorities.

One day, in frustration at our lack of cross-cultural friendships, my husband, Paul, and I decided to write down every network in which we interacted. We counted fifteen groups that didn't overlap and noticed most of our friends looked and lived just like us. Once we saw this written down in front of us, we determined to make creative changes to consolidate, concentrate, and then expand our spheres of influence.

> WE WILL NEED TO SAY NO TO VERY GOOD THINGS IN ORDER TO SAY YES TO THE VERY BEST THINGS.

We exchanged our traditional small group at church for a like-minded group that wanted to reach out to internationals. This allowed us to interact with believing friends *and* internationals at the same time—and created a valuable accountability and team structure to do what we said we would do. I traded serving on the worship team at church for leading a team to serve refugees. Church leaders blessed this outward-facing team, and the people in our spheres of influence gradually shifted. Refugee work gave us a natural reason to be with our new friends from Iraq, Saudi Arabia, and India.

TRY IT!

Write down all your spheres of influence or your networks, circle them, and see which ones overlap. Mark which spheres of influence give you access to people from the cultures you wish to befriend. Brainstorm how you can combine some of the groups. If circles can't overlap, ask God to show you which activities should stop for a season, especially ones that don't include multicultural friendships. Then you can focus on making new habits that put you in cross-cultural contexts as a more regular, integrated part of your schedule.

Habit #2: Plan "unplanned" time.

It's easy to feel trapped by our filled-up calendars and never have downtime or be available to get to know our multicultural friends in a relaxed setting, or at a last-minute opportunity. There's a natural tension at play, especially when our new friends come from a culture where it's more normal to show up unannounced or to contact someone just before coming than to call days or weeks ahead of time.

When we lived in India, our doorbell rang at least twenty times a day, the present urgency always overriding any premade plans. One time, at 6:00 a.m., a friend called my husband.

"Where are you?" he asked.

"I'm sleeping!"

"Oh. Can I come use your shower? My wife and I have been at the hospital with my mother-in-law for three days now, and your house is nearby."

"Of course," said Paul.

"Okay, very good. We are at your door right now."

One way to navigate this difference in mind-set is to capitalize on our Western need to plan by blocking off specific time as unplanned time. This forces us to create the space to be unplanned—and to be available to Eastern-culture friends for a few hours, or a day together, not just a few minutes. What this looked like in my life was setting aside a day each week for my refugee friends. I resisted making specific plans with them but guarded my schedule on those days to create space for them. That way I could respond to anything a friend wanted to do that day. We might learn to ride the bus system, go to the library, or cook a special dish they happened to be making.

It's important to know when to schedule these unplanned times, so our cross-cultural friends will naturally be available too. In India, people work six days a week and take Sundays off. Therefore, weddings, family gatherings, and visits to home villages occur on Sundays. It took a few months for us to recognize the need to switch our day of worship and rest—our Sabbath and our family day—to Saturday. Once we did this, we were able to leave our Sundays open as unplanned time, so we could be available when our local friends expected to have leisure time.

TRY IT!

Take a calendar, and color in blocks, showing how you generally spend your days each week. Include time spent on things such as social media and regular television shows. Notice which activities take up chunks of space but bring little value to your emotional, spiritual, or physical well-being, and make a plan to cut them out. Write in when you'll spend extended time with God. Write in planned "unplanned" areas, intentionally blocking off parts of your calendar to be with people from other cultures. If you already live overseas, you will aim for a much higher percentage of your time in these categories.

Habit #3: Eat together.

At our church here in America, the main worship area houses spaces with different types of seating: pews to symbolize the value of tradition, plastic chairs to remind us that we're not meant to stay comfortable, and couches to symbolize that Jesus provides rest. Two handmade, large, oak farm tables also grace the seating area, meant to symbolize the biblical practice of sharing lives and sharing food around a table.[5]

Eating together is a powerful way to solidify friendship and brings relationships to a new level, even more so when done in someone's home. In Western cultures we might meet friends at a restaurant, but rarely do we invite another family over for dinner just because. What we miss out on, though, is the intimacy and depth of relationship that comes when we sit around the table in the places we call home, talking, laughing, and taking our time.

In Eastern cultures, nothing worth doing is done without being centered around food. In fact, serving others the best food available is a sign of great honor. Once, while visiting some Bedouins in Africa, I petted a cute little goat bleating and butting the sides of the tent. That night, the unlucky goat appeared on the central platter as the main event, a delicacy reserved for special occasions and special guests.

Though I was both surprised and a little bit heartbroken at this, I knew that our hosts had served us their goat to show respect and honor to us.

We see King David do the same thing in the Bible when he wanted to show honor to his dear friend Jonathan after his death. He determined he would do so by caring for and honoring Jonathan's son Mephibosheth. How did he show him honor? Let's look at what he said in 2 Samuel: "'I will give you all the property that once belonged to your grandfather Saul, and you will eat here with me at the king's table!' . . . And from that time on, Mephibosheth ate regularly at David's table, like one of the king's own sons" (2 Sam. 9:7, 11).

Keeping in mind the significance of coming to the table together regularly, my outreach-focused small group decided to put this into practice by rotating who provided dinner for everyone. Learning to cook for twenty or thirty people, on a budget, stretched my imagination and culinary capabilities—not a strong area of mine! Later, though, while living in India, I realized how that season of cooking for crowds prepared me for living in another culture. People there expected tasty food, often made completely from scratch, for many people. Although not an easy task, it was both an honor for me to serve in this way and an honor I could show for the people God had brought into our lives.

TRY IT!

Invite a neighbor or a coworker and his or her family from another country over to your house for dinner this week. Research the kinds of food that will not offend them, and tell them ahead of time what you'll serve. For example, a Hindu will eat vegetarian, and a Muslim will not eat pork.

> Serve your very best meal that costs you something in time and resources and might include a trip to an ethnic grocery store. Or, if you don't know someone from another culture yet, choose someone you've never invited to your home before. Watch how eating together brings you closer together.

Habit #4: Cultivate extreme hospitality.

The idea of extreme hospitality—giving your very best time, food, focus, and attention to all who cross the threshold of your home—isn't natural to Westerners, especially in the context of offering it to strangers. Often, we are much too practical, busy, and wrapped up in our individual agendas to be hospitable in this lavish way. But for Eastern cultures, it's almost a given.

Because of the emphasis on family networks, interdependence, living in community, and people preference over project preference, there is a sense that nothing is too good for a guest. And nothing else in the schedule is as important as a guest. Visitors to most Eastern countries can expect invitations to tea in someone's home, even though they are strangers.

Most field-workers learn this quickly and wouldn't think of relegating a visitor to a hotel, whether they're in their host country or in their home country. No matter how humble their living conditions, if there is a spot on the floor, there is room for one more. This is a mind-set we'd be wise to cultivate as we reorient our lives toward people of other cultures.

TRY IT!

Practice extreme hospitality by inviting a family you are not related to over for an overnight visit or weekend with your family, in your home. Tell them you're trying to practice communal living. Another idea is to ask your church to let you host the next field-worker coming through town. Or, the next time your family is planning a vacation, rent a cabin in the woods with a few others to save money and practice cooking and living together. As you begin to let others into your everyday lives, notice what areas of communal living are difficult for you and where you need to let go of selfishness, personal space, and private time.

Habit #5: Go with the flow.

Westerners value punctuality. We expect people to be on time, and we have well-planned infrastructures that support that expectation, making it possible to plan something and expect it will happen when we said it would. Not so in many other countries. People in other cultures understand that things happen—floods, traffic, the train breaks down, the grandmother gets sick, or a friend stops by for tea. Setting a time for an event to start is simply a guideline, with the greater value on making sure everyone gets there who is supposed to be there. Once everyone arrives, the event starts, no matter if it's hours later than planned.

After moving from the Philippines, where I grew up, to America to attend university, I realized I was always late. I still am! Once, an American took me aside and told me gravely that my lateness showed great disrespect to the other person, and she likened it to a sin. I had no idea! In fact, whenever someone showed up early to something I planned, I felt *she* was being disrespectful. Because, of course, I wouldn't be ready, and I'd become flustered and stressed. That's why, as we interact with friends from other cultures, it's a good guideline to be less strict about time, to learn flexibility.

In cultures where anything can happen without notice, it's also helpful to learn to hold expectations lightly and grow adept at coming up with alternate plans. On my daughter's sixteenth birthday in India, we gathered our friends into *tuk-tuks*, motorcycles with sidecars, to ride across town and see the only English-language movie showing in the only theater in town. When we got there, we learned that all the theaters in the state were closed because of a strike against something. We shrugged it off and walked over to a salon to get pedicures instead. Sorry! Only men get pedicures in this town. We chuckled a bit and walked across the busy street to a stall selling English-language movies on DVDs. But when we got home, we discovered they were pirated DVDs that wouldn't play on our laptop. So we made popcorn on the stove and downloaded a movie online. Sorry! It would take twenty-two hours to download it because of the slow internet. We rolled our eyes and found a DVD we hadn't watched in a while and turned it on. But it turned out it had gotten chewed up by the humidity and stalled every ten minutes.

We finally piled into the one room with an air conditioner unit and stayed up late talking, telling stories, and having a sleepover shoulder to shoulder, laughing and bonding over our series of unfortunate events until tears rolled down our cheeks. My daughter won't ever forget *that* birthday!

TRY IT!

This week, choose the longest line at the grocery store to check out. Take the longest route to work or school. Plan something with the family, and then completely change it five minutes before. Then, when you get to where you're going, completely change it again. When doing something with your multicultural friends and things don't go as planned or don't happen when they are planned, tell yourself it's all part of the journey and you're learning cultural flexibility.

Habit #6: Honor everyone, and don't bring public shame on anyone.

In Eastern cultures, honor is more important than anything else. Shame ruins everything. If people lose honor in public, they bring shame on themselves—and their families. Because Eastern cultures operate on a communal rather than an individual worldview, the shame brought on an individual also extends to the individual's entire family line. If someone does something illegal and he or she doesn't get caught, then it may not be considered wrong. No one knows about it but God, and he will forgive. But once someone gets caught and is publicly humiliated, this is when it is perceived as wrong.

For example, little Vijay steals a candy bar from the local store. His parents take it from him and throw it away, scolding him and warning that if he keeps doing things like this, he will get caught. Then everyone will think his whole family is untrustworthy, and they won't be able to buy from that store any longer.

Eastern families go to great lengths to protect the family name from shame. Marrying beneath one's social position, pregnancy out of wedlock, converting to Christianity and thus aligning oneself with Western values (or lack thereof), disagreeing with a family decision made by the patriarch—these things are unthinkable to Eastern families, and they will not allow it.

Honor and shame drives Eastern society, from business, to marriage, to religion, and everything in between. So when entering an Eastern culture, everything you do—everything you are—*must* promote and protect the honor of the family. Practically, this looks like honoring everyone who is older than you by letting them go first, doing it their way, and asking their counsel. Try not to publicly correct anyone, which humiliates them in front of others. And it's a good idea to get permission from the family patriarch or matriarch before introducing any kind of change, even when interacting with them in your own culture.

TRY IT!

In your home, try letting the oldest person in the room sit first, eat first, enter the car first, and make the decision about what you'll do that evening. Anytime you greet your cross-cultural friends, ask them, "How are your mother and father?" And if you are tempted to disagree with someone in a group setting, hold your tongue, smile and nod, and talk to them another time, alone, about your differing opinion. Notice how lifted up the person you are serving feels.

A Changed Couple

After several years of practicing the principles in this chapter in their own city, Joel and Hannah eventually moved overseas. They recently visited America after having been gone a few years, and we invited them to stay in our home for a couple of days.

Joel and Hannah arrived four hours later than planned, breezing in the front door with one small suitcase to last the whole family for the weekend. The children crashed all in one room on the floor that night while Joel, Hannah, my husband, and I stayed up late talking and catching up.

They told us about all the friends they'd made overseas, the spiritual conversations they had every day, and talked about how many of the habits they'd practiced in their cross-cultural missional group here in America had helped prepare them for the realities of life in an Eastern culture.

I smiled to myself, thinking how far they'd come, and breathed thanks to God for honoring their intentional lifestyle changes and their openness to entering other cultures well, blessing them with fruitfulness in their cross-cultural context.

Reflection

1. Think of someone you know who grew up in different country. How are your concepts of things such as time, decision-making, hospitality, family involvement, and personal space different from his or hers?

2. Which of the four cultural tips for entering a new cultural situation might be easiest for you to apply? Which would be hardest? Why?

3. Which of the six habits of cultural practice would be easiest for you to try? Which would be the hardest? Why?

4. How could you upgrade your personal interactions with people from other cultures to honor them?

THREE

Engaging International Students
and Welcoming Refugees

Chongan, an engineering student from China, walked off a Singapore Airlines flight into the bustle of Los Angeles International Airport. A crisp Dodgers T-shirt peeked out from under his name-brand leather jacket, matching the red of his rolling suitcase. He stopped to read the signs for baggage claim, excited and nervous about his first trip to America to study at the University of California–Los Angeles.

Just when it looked as if the plane had emptied, a family of four emerged from the exit ramp. A young mother from Somalia wearing a head covering and a brown wool dress reaching the floor clutched a bag and two small children. Jamilah paused and glanced around.

Both Chongan and the family walked past security, looking ahead to their future. Jamilah nodded in relief when she saw a caseworker with the refugee agency step forward holding a card with her name on it. Behind the caseworker, a group of smiling Americans stood holding red, white, and blue balloons and waving signs that read, "Welcome to America!"

Chongan watched as a few women, an older gentleman, a teenager, and two younger children encircled the Somali family, nodding smiles, saying vigorous hellos, and giving out juice boxes to the children hiding behind their mother's skirt. He thought of all the American friends he might make and the American food he'd try. He felt sure he would have adventurous, fun stories to tell his friends and family back home about how well he fared in this new country of opportunity.

The "Comers"

When we think about reaching the nations, we often think of those who *go* to the places and peoples with the least access to Jesus Christ. However, people with the least access to Jesus also *come* to places where Jesus followers live. International students like Chongan and refugees like Jamilah come from unreached people groups, those with less than 2 percent of Christians among them. They come to Christian nations and then have access to the gospel.

Throughout history God has used four situations to introduce unreached peoples to the good news of Jesus Christ: Christians going to them, both willingly and unwillingly, and the peoples coming to where Christians are—both willingly, like international students, and unwillingly, like refugees.[1]

For those of us not currently traveling overseas, these comers showing up on our doorsteps as our new neighbors is such a gift. It's an opportunity for us to welcome them well, to obey Jesus by inviting the foreigner into our homes (see Matt. 25:35). With love and respect, we can eventually encourage them to follow Christ. This also allows us to practice forming intentional relationships with international friends, which is helpful should we eventually travel overseas. Let's dig in a little deeper to understanding both international students like Chongan and refugees like Jamilah, so we can walk across the street to the nations coming to us.

Willingly

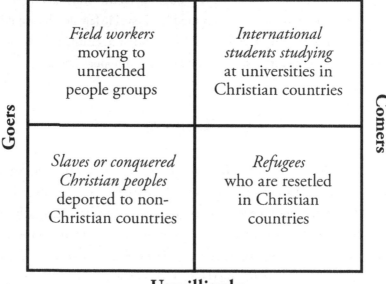

| Goers | Field workers moving to unreached people groups | International students studying at universities in Christian countries | Comers |
| | Slaves or conquered Christian peoples deported to non-Christian countries | Refugees who are resetled in Christian countries | |

Unwillingly

International Students

Out of the world's four million international students, almost a million study at American universities, half a million in the United Kingdom, and a quarter million in Australia. Nearly half of all international students who study abroad come from China and India—with South Korea and Saudi Arabia sending the next largest representations.[2]

High concentrations of people without access to Jesus Christ live in China, India, and Saudi Arabia—coming from nonreligious, Hindu, and Muslim backgrounds. Astonishingly, almost 60 percent of all international students come from countries where the Christian population is less than 2 percent. Students, like Chongan, are willingly showing up at a university near us, eager to make a new Western friend!

This offers us the chance to shape an international student's under-standing of Jesus Christ, impacting the kind of people who will one day shape their countries. Students like Chongan come from wealthy, influential families and return to their home countries as leaders, changemakers, and policy shapers. Ben Wolfgang, in a *Washington Times* article, pointed out that "a surprising number of politicians, dip-lomats, lawmakers, military leaders and business tycoons from around the globe—in countries both friendly and hostile—have spent time in U.S. colleges and universities." In fact, in 2005, the United States worked to negotiate a deal to end a decades-long war between Sudan and South Sudan. A guerrilla fighter leading the southern resistance collaborated with the United States in the peace process. His name? Mohamed Morsi. Wolfgang wrote, "Long before Mohamed Morsi rose through the ranks of Egypt's Muslim Brotherhood to win the country's post-revolution presidential election, he was a Trojan at the University of Southern California earning a doctorate in engineering from the Los Angeles school."[3]

On the other side of things, there have also been students who didn't come out of their experience as positively. Several of the al-Qaeda terrorists from the 9/11 attack also studied in America as international students.[4] What if a follower of Jesus had invited them into their home then, sitting eye to eye across the dinner table and offering love, peace, and friendship? Could interactions like this have painted a more compelling and accurate portrait of Americans—and of Christ followers—than the brainwashed portrayal that often comes from Islamic fundamentalists? Befriending international students is indeed a strategic opportunity.

These students are within reach of the gospel for just a few short years. We don't have much time to show them the kingdom of God, with its wealth of riches that has nothing to do with the money, power, and prestige they seek but everything to do with the satisfaction, purpose, and peace they need. So, we would be wise to steward the time that we do have with them well.

Connecting with an International Student

INTERNATIONAL STUDENTS ARE WITHIN REACH OF THE GOSPEL FOR JUST A FEW SHORT YEARS.

As Chongan watched the Somali family getting their welcome, a young man wearing shorts and a T-shirt tapped him on the shoulder. He held a sign labeled "UCLA" with Chongan's name on it.

"Hi! Are you Chongan?" asked Brian, a student. "I'm here from the university to drive you to your dorm." Chongan didn't miss a beat. He spoke fluent English and knew enough about Western cultures from television and movies. He smiled broadly and shook Brian's hand. They chatted the whole way to baggage claim about the trip and his university plans.

"Do you want to stop and get something to eat before I drop you off at your dorm room? How about I introduce you to a great fast-food place that a lot of people like, called Chick-fil-A?" suggested Brian.

They spent the next few hours eating, talking about food, common interests, and their families. Chongan's mother called him via video chat on his cell phone, and he proudly introduced her to Brian, who said a few words of greeting. He zoomed the video for his mother all around Chick-fil-A so she could see what America looked like. Chongan gave Brian a good look at his family's home too—a two-thousand-square-foot, exquisitely furnished flat on the fourth floor.

As Brian parked at the university dorms, he and Chongan exchanged phone numbers, and he said, "You'll have to come over and meet my wife sometime! Maybe when you need a break from school or something. We don't live too far from here. If you need anything as you're getting settled in, we're happy to answer any questions. How about if I check in with you in a couple of days and see how you're doing?"

Chongan felt a sense of relief that he now knew someone personally in this new country.

Faith-based on-campus organizations make it easy for any one of us to connect with students like Chongan. And when churches get involved, more believers get involved. One church in a small, rural city in Kansas serves hundreds of international students attending a local university. In addition to providing practical help, like airport and grocery runs and English conversation classes, they also host on-campus Bible studies and offer a special young-adults class on Sundays geared toward students from other countries.

Let's fast-forward through years of friendship between Chongan and Brian and his wife to see what God did. Chongan and his brother, who also came to the United States, eventually chose to follow Jesus, while Brian discipled them. Brian baptized Chongan, and Chongan baptized his brother on the same day in an emotional celebration. Chongan and his brother returned to China to work and led most of their extended family to Jesus. Ten years later, Chongan flew Brian and his wife to China—all expenses paid—to meet his family and attend his wedding in a happy reunion of old friends.

The nations are coming to our doorsteps too, and we and our churches have the joy and opportunity to befriend them.

WAYS TO BEFRIEND INTERNATIONAL STUDENTS

- Sign up to be an international friend at your local university (training and coaching are usually provided)

- Open your home to students for a holiday meal
- Attend cultural events at a university campus
- Volunteer to pick students up at the airport on arrival
- Organize fun group events to see sites in your state
- Be a family away from home, and invite them over when they get lonely
- Provide transportation to and from the grocery store
- Participate in (or start) conversational English classes on campus
- Befriend international women by hosting a tea party at your home
- Invite them to read the Bible with you!

We can make a difference even today if we would open our hearts to the people God is bringing. Let's take a moment to pray for the international students studying around the world right now:

Lord, please show yourself to international students as they experience new things and new ideas in countries with open freedom to worship you. Provide a true follower of Jesus to befriend every student that enters my country. They have something they didn't have before—access to Jesus Christ and the treasures of the kingdom of God.

Show yourself to them through me. May they see Christ in me, as I obey you by loving them; learning about their lives, countries, and families; and listening to their hopes, dreams, and struggles. Open my heart to discover specific ways I can be their friend.

Refugees

A world crisis continues to escalate. Millions of people flee war, persecution, and violence in their home countries. The number of people on the run from violence in the world today is staggering—and only getting worse. Sixty-five million people, a population greater than all of France, lived forcibly displaced from their homes as of 2015—a number twice as high as ten years before. Distressingly, children make up 50 percent of these numbers, with thousands arriving in their host countries without an adult. One out of every 113 people on the planet live as internally displaced persons (those fleeing within their own borders) or refugees (those fleeing outside their borders, qualifying for refugee status).[5]

The Old Testament is full of stories of God's people also in desperate circumstances. Many cried out to God for help. In turn, God called them to come home to him. But displaced people and refugees fleeing in our time come from countries that are majority Muslim, Buddhist, or formerly Communist. They don't have a history of knowing the love of God, or the call to come back him.

And the need is great and growing. Who will step up to meet it? *We* must go to the people in places of pain and suffering to both serve them in their physical needs and to guide them to the source of all help, healing, comfort, and restoration. As hurting people cry out like this to God, let's be the answer to their cries, as it says in the Psalms, "But in my distress I cried out to the LORD; yes, I prayed to my God for help. He heard me from his sanctuary; my cry to him reached his ears" (18:6). But before we can serve them, we need to know them and their situation a little better.

Who are the forty-one million internally displaced persons?

We sometimes get confused and call everyone forced to flee his or her home a refugee. But a greater number of people fleeing actually haven't crossed an international border, are still within their own countries, and thus are not officially "refugees." They are called *internally displaced persons* (IDPs). Although they are also forced to flee their homes because of war, persecution, or violence, they aren't protected by international law or eligible to receive aid, so they are some of the most vulnerable populations in the world, and few people know about them. IDPs don't show up on Western shores and greatly need our prayers and aid from private nonprofits.

The highest numbers of internally displaced persons are in Columbia, Syria, and Iraq, where there are numerous horrific stories of people fleeing for survival.[6] Care, a private humanitarian organization providing relief in critical areas of the world, reports that in Yemen fifteen million people are in danger of running out of water, and eight million people are starving because of ongoing violence in the country. This forced two and a half million people to flee their homes, while still remaining inside the country's borders.[7] We just don't hear enough about these situations on the Western news. We can get informed by researching international aid organizations, following them on social media, and financially and prayerfully supporting them in relief efforts.

Who are the twenty-one million refugees?

Refugees are people who've crossed international borders, seeking asylum, who have successfully proven their fears of persecution, war, or violence—usually based on race, religion, nationality, or political opinion—are well-founded. It's little understood that people who flee because of natural disasters or economic troubles aren't actually eligible for refugee status, so the people showing up on the shores of democratic countries are running for their lives, with emotional and physical scars, as victims of violence. Most of the world's refugees today come from three countries: Syria, Afghanistan, and Somalia. In fact, as of 2017, more than five million people crossed international borders to flee the war in Syria, and they're still fleeing.[8]

How do some refugees end up in majority Christian countries?

Half of the world's refugees or those seeking asylum are found in the ten countries closest to troubled nations. Countries such as Jordan, Turkey, Pakistan, and Lebanon each shelter several million people displaced from their homeland.[9] Refugees who can't return to their home countries, and who aren't expected to do well in their host countries, can apply to the United Nations High Commissioner for Refugees (UNHCR) to be resettled in a third country.

Being approved for refugee resettlement is like winning the lottery. Third-country resettlement only becomes an option when all efforts to help refugees return home or settle permanently in their country of asylum have failed. Only 1 percent of those who apply get this chance.[10] For example, the United States—one of the countries that accepts the most resettled refugees—only welcomes fifty thousand new refugees per year. This represents a mere .002 percent of the entire refugee population.[11]

With the exception of Japan, countries that offer resettlement all have significant Christian populations: Australia, Canada, Denmark, Finland, the Netherlands, New Zealand, Norway, Sweden, Switzerland, and the United States, among others.[12] So while the reality of us traveling to Yemen or Syria isn't likely right now, some of the people from those places are coming to us. Mostly women and children, victims of unimaginable trauma arrive every day at an airport near us, looking for safety and a friendly face.

What can we do to step into this need with God's love? This next section will help us see what it looks like to interact well in our home country with those who have been granted refugee resettlement status.

A Biblical Perspective on Welcoming the Foreigner

Heidi, an American single mother of two teenagers, worked a full-time job and lived in a suburb of a city in America. After she caught God's heart for the nations on a short-term trip, she looked around to see how she could reach the world right where she lived. She contacted the local refugee resettlement branch in her area, filled out a volunteer application, and attended training on welcoming refugees. Then Heidi met with her church leaders and invited the church, as well as her coworkers, to join her in welcoming a refugee family.

Genie, a practical, get-it-done person who heard about Heidi's plans at church, started collecting donated items to furnish an apartment for a family. Genie's garage filled up quickly with a bunk bed, mattresses, a couch set, a dining-room table, kitchen appliances, and children's toys.

In a few weeks, the volunteer coordinator at the refugee resettlement agency called Heidi and said, "We have a single mother with two small children scheduled to arrive from Somalia this Thursday at 7:15 p.m. Can you have the apartment ready by then and meet them at the airport?" Yes!

Heidi and her team members cleared their schedules and met at the apartment where the refugee resettlement agency would house the new family. The group spent the evening moving furniture, and Heidi returned the next day with her teenage daughter to hang curtains and pictures. Another family offered to buy enough groceries to stock the kitchen for a week. They visited an Islamic grocery store for the first time to buy halal[1] chicken for their new Muslim friends.

That's how the group ended up on Thursday night at the airport with welcome signs, balloons, and treats to greet Jamilah and her children. An Arabic-speaking social worker from the refugee resettlement agency translated as the group greeted the travel-weary but grateful Jamilah. They picked up two duffel bags from baggage claim—everything she owned in the world—and drove to the furnished apartment.

The group showed Jamilah how to operate the stove, the microwave, and even the thermostat—all new things to her. Eventually, they lured the young children out from hiding behind their mother's skirt with a few matchbox cars. Heidi asked if she could pray a blessing over the new home and the family, and Jamilah lifted her hands, palms up, to God. The whole group crowded into the tiny kitchen to give thanks and joined Jamilah with palms up, eyes looking to the heavens.

But the adventure wasn't over. The next day would be more confusing than the first for Jamilah. Heidi's team decided who would visit the family and when, so that someone checked in on her regularly for the next few months.

Heidi visited the next day with the caseworker and learned part of Jamilah's story. Al-Qaeda terrorists had killed her husband and her oldest son in a raid. The caseworker told how Jamilah, barely nineteen at the time, since she married at twelve years old, strapped her baby to her front and her toddler on her back. She set off on foot across a

---

1 *Halal* means "acceptable" or "clean." Muslims believe animals should be killed in a certain way, which makes it acceptable for them to eat. Most ethnic grocery stores in Western countries will sell halal meat.

dangerous and difficult path, traversing more than a hundred miles until she reached a refugee camp in Uganda.

After this visit, moved by the mother's story, Heidi started praying for Jamilah every day. When team members visited the family, they showed Jamilah how to use the city bus and how to check out books at the library. One time, they took the kids to the zoo. Jamilah only knew a little bit of English, so Genie even started holding English classes a few times a week at the apartment complex. Eventually, Jamilah learned enough to get a job at the airport, cleaning, while her children attended preschool. She often thanked her friends for their love and a new start.

Welcoming people from other countries, much as Heidi and her friends did for Jamilah, is a deeply biblical practice. Jesus says, "For I was hungry, and you fed me. I was thirsty, and you gave me a drink. I was a stranger [also translated "foreigner"], and you invited me into your home" (Matt. 25:35). Jesus himself was a refugee. Joseph and Mary fled with baby Jesus to seek asylum in Egypt from Roman oppression (Matt. 2:13).

Numerous references in the Old Testament also highlight God's concern for foreigners living under Israel's protection (Lev 19:9–10, 33–34; Jer. 7:5–7, and dozens more).[13] Moses said that God "shows love to the foreigners living among you and gives them food and clothing. So you, too, must show love to foreigners" (Deut. 10:18–19). In the same breath that the Lord expressed concern for the oppression of widows, orphans, and the poor, he also expressed concern for the oppression of foreigners (Zech. 7:10). Ruth found favor as a foreigner (Ruth 2:11) and ended up being in the family line of Jesus.

Unfortunately, the real threat of terrorism, combined with ignorance and prejudice about refugee resettlement, often fosters a climate of fear regarding refugees and tempts us to forget the way God views them. But if we seek to be faithful to God's heart for the foreigner, then what can we do when we feel afraid? Combat fear with facts. Combat fear with understanding. And combat fear with love.

#1: Combat fear with facts.

Refugees are among the most vetted foreigners to enter countries approved for refugee resettlement—more than tourists, international students, and immigrants. There are much easier and more logical ways to enter a country with ill intentions than to submit oneself to years of probing by the UNHCR.

For those fortunate enough to be resettled in a third country, it takes an average of eighteen to twenty-four months—sometimes longer—to walk through the rigorous applications, background checks, and approval systems. The US Department of State wrote, "Nothing is more important to us than the security of the American people. The United States remains deeply committed to safeguarding the American people, just as we are committed to providing refuge to the world's most vulnerable people. These goals are not mutually exclusive."[14]

#2: Combat fear with understanding.

Refugees are people like us—who want the same things we want. Al, who was once forced to flee Iraq and is now a volunteer with refugee resettlement agency World Relief, says that "refugees want . . . peace, freedom and safety. They want to contribute to their new community. They are fleeing the same type of violence that you are afraid of, and they care about the refugee program being safe and secure, just like US citizens do. Above all, they want to build a good life for themselves and their families, and hope for good things for future generations."[15]

If we can view refugees arriving in our country as moms and dads, brothers and sisters, with children and hopes for their good future, we'll view them with more humanity than the media might portray.

#3: Combat fear with love.

Love dissipates fear. In a world fraught with unimaginable violence, most of us—quite understandably—fear for the safety our country. But some aim this natural fear at other cultures, worried that foreigners will upset the freedoms they enjoy. This self-protection can turn into an unhealthy revulsion of other cultures and keep us from living out love. Some Christians who go to church regularly, read their Bibles, and profess to follow Jesus, also forward emails filled with fear, inspiring more fear. They contain hateful words about Muslims and, most recently, Muslim refugees. If you get one of those emails, delete it.

The apostle John said, "God is love, and all who live in love live in God, and God lives in them. And as we live in God, our love grows more perfect. . . . Such love has no fear, because perfect love expels all fear. If we are afraid, it is for fear of punishment, and this shows that we have not fully experienced his perfect love" (1 John 4:16–18).

Love compels us to move beyond our fear and obey God's Word. If we wear love as our clothing in every interaction, it will change our perspective.

Five Ways to Love Refugees Well

Do you feel ready to welcome a refugee in your country? Making friends with people recovering from trauma requires sensitivity, understanding, and patience. Here are a few things to remember to help you on your way:

#1: Help refugees keep their dignity.

Most resettled refugees I know don't like to be called refugees. It sounds "less than" and labels them as needy and helpless. While many do come from situations of poverty or from years living in refugee camps, other refugees left behind affluent and comfortable lives. Those from Iraq and Syria, the two countries producing some of the highest numbers of refugees today, are mostly educated. Many Iraqi and Syrian refugees owned homes, land, and businesses before they fled. Ahmed, an Iraqi gentleman in his midfifties, owned several hotels in his country. But because he cannot yet speak English, he now washes dishes at a Marriott resort for a living. Most Westerners who meet him would have no idea of his capabilities or his experience in leadership and business.

LOVE COMPELS US TO MOVE BEYOND OUR FEAR AND OBEY GOD'S WORD. IF WE WEAR LOVE AS OUR CLOTHING IN EVERY INTERACTION, IT WILL CHANGE OUR PERSPECTIVE.

Whether we're working with people who come from affluence or from poverty, recognize and affirm the assets and experience they bring to their new countries, instead of only considering what they need for survival. Yes, they may struggle with language or be confused about how things work in the new country, but that doesn't mean they don't have much to offer.

We can look for ways refugees can help us and others around them, rather than always being the one to help them. Hajer, my widow friend from chapter 1, owned a hair salon in her home country. One day she looked at me, with no makeup and my hair pulled back in a ponytail, and said, "I can make you beautiful." So I let her try! She gave me a complete makeover, including a new hairstyle, highlights, and eyebrow waxing. For years she cut my hair as I encouraged her to start her own salon business out of her home, making business cards for her and providing start-up supplies.

#2: Give refugees time, friendship, and resources to heal emotionally.

Since the very definition of *refugee* implies that a person has fled a form of persecution or violence, most refugees have experienced trauma. Much happens inside the soul, mind, and heart when trauma occurs. Even as refugees enter a new country with hopes for safety and freedom, they also arrive with deep loss and suffering in their past. They've lost people, homes, and dreams, in addition to possibly having experienced rape, torture, slavery, and other unimaginable horrors.

As you make friends with refugees, give them space and plenty of relational time over tea to trust you. Telling one's story can be part of the healing. Let them talk only if they want to talk. Don't try to solve anything or explain anything. Just listen. Pray. And when it seems right, guide them to resources that will help them heal and process their past.[16]

#3: Show them the ropes in their new country.

It's confusing to enter a new culture. What do you do when you're sick? Even setting up a doctor's appointment is different in a new country, let alone managing insurance. How do you get from one place to another? If you don't own a car, as is the case with most refugees, you'd need to learn to use public transportation. How do you get rid of carrot peelings? In many places, people feed food scraps to animals and have never even heard of garbage disposals. How and where do you sign up your child for school? Where should you shop, and what stores give the best deals?

Every time we visit a refugee family's apartment in the first few months, even the first few years, we can ask, "Do you have a question about how to do anything?" Chances are, they'll ask us to help browse through jobs on Monster.com, translate for a doctor's appointment, or do laundry together as we show them the convenience of using a dryer. Don't assume anything. Many things are new and confusing.

#4: Empower refugees instead of enabling them.

In my experience, Westerners feel pretty good about furnishing an entire apartment for a new refugee family. And it makes them want to keep giving more things. It's okay to furnish an apartment at first, because the family comes with nothing. But after that first day, don't become a source for stuff. When our new friends know that we furnished the apartment and we are always asking them if they need anything else, we become a funnel for free things—instead of becoming a friend.

The goal with new refugee families is not to make them dependent on us or the welfare system or anyone else. Help them be successful on their own. For example, Heidi noticed that Jamilah didn't have a stroller for her youngest child. Heidi knew she could get a free one donated within an hour. But she didn't do the easy thing. She did what was best for the mother, even though it took more time. She visited Jamilah and explained how a stroller worked and how it might help her get around easier since she had to walk to most places. Then she walked with her to a nearby Goodwill store.

Heidi let Jamilah in on the secret about where to find gently used items available at inexpensive prices in secondhand stores. Then, instead of choosing a stroller, Jamilah explained through hand motions that she's used to carrying her babies. Heidi helped her find a cloth front carrier that she loved much more than the stroller. Jamilah felt a surge of honor as she carefully took a few dollars out of her small allowance from the refugee resettlement agency to pay for the carrier herself.

Heidi became a peer and a friend—not the "wealthy savior" providing for the "needy poor." She suggested that Jamilah tell her other Somali friends in the apartment complex about the nearby Goodwill. She did, much to her friends' delight and relief.

#5: Be a friend.

People entering a new country need a friend most of all. They want to belong. They need someone to be available in emergencies—and to know that someone cares about them.

Invite refugee friends over to your home for a meal. Introduce them to others in your network. Include children, or college roommates, or other friends, when you plan outings with them. Laugh. Make it fun. Take them bowling. Ask them to teach you how to cook a special dish from their country. Go shopping together. Pray for and with them. Be a friend.

Do We Still Need to Go to the Nations If They're Coming Here?

Yes. Yes. Yes! Let's keep the big picture in mind. Out of one million international students in America, about 60 percent are from unreached people groups. That's 600,000 students. But imagine the 204 million people in unreached people groups waiting back home—in just one state of one country!

Let the magnitude of those numbers sink in. In Uttar Pradesh, India, where only one-fifth of 1 percent of the population identify as Christian, there are 204 million Hindus and Muslims, 340 times the number of international students in America from all the unreached people groups. To make the imbalance more stark, in Arizona, where about 20,000 international students study, Christians from about 250 evangelical churches worship.[17] Only a handful of field-workers live in Uttar Pradesh, trying to reach the 204 million people without access to Jesus!

So, *yes*, somebody still needs to go where the need is greatest.

Remember: while America settles the third-largest number of refugees, the numbers are comparatively so small—only .002 percent of the global refugee population. Welcoming a refugee family is a great place to start for those who are pursuing God's heart for the nations. This is a beautiful, strategic, obedient thing to do as Christ's followers. But there is so much more opportunity outside our own countries.

Imagine the opportunities to love refugees in countries situated closer to war, persecution, and violence. For example, an entire town of more than one hundred thousand people from unreached people groups in Sudan fled to South Sudan, a fledgling democracy with freedom of religion.

A field-worker team moved there to help in practical ways. They provided education for children and improved temporary living conditions. With love and respect, they also invited hurting people to find true freedom from their oppression through Jesus Christ. Bible studies started like wildfire through the camps. The people, desperate for healing in their souls, responded to Jesus Christ openly and freely as allegiance and obedience to Jesus and his ways spread throughout the camps. People experienced physical and emotional healing. They gave and received forgiveness. Families walked through grief with the Holy Spirit as comforter. The transformation was so startling, the mayor asked the field workers for more people like them to come and start more of these groups, reading and obeying the Bible.

There aren't enough people willing to go, and the opportunity still stands. There are people and places wide open for followers of Jesus to come and love the most vulnerable.

Let's pray for the millions of people enduring unimaginable suffering around the world, and those coming to our doorstep:

Lord, give us a compassionate heart like yours. Please come to the rescue of little children, men, and women forced to flee their homes and country. We pray for your justice, your shelter, and your protection over them. As they cry for help to you, please answer them. And if part of that answer includes me, please show me who I can advocate for, where I can give, and how I can welcome and love them right where I am.

Reflection

1. How has your perception of international students changed? What are strategic and spiritual reasons to make an international student friend?
2. How has your perception of refugees changed? What is the difference between internally displaced persons and refugees?
3. What is God asking you to do in response to what you've read in this chapter?

FOUR

Cultivating Intentional Cross-Cultural Disciples

Sometimes, we make cross-cultural friends and interact with them for a long time without engaging in deep spiritual conversations or reading the Bible together. We hope someday our non-believing friends will notice something different about us and ask us to explain. Most of the time, that day never comes. We might salt our friendships with a prayer now and then, but nothing spiritually significant seems to happen.

I've been there! But with Ayisha, my friend from chapter 1, I determined to try something different. After about a year of friendship, doing life together, praying and discussing stories of Jesus sometimes, we seemed to be good friends on a spiritual treadmill going nowhere. So, I decided to intentionally invite her into a discipleship relationship. Here's how it happened.

One evening, as we chatted and sampled all her favorite foods at a local ethnic restaurant, Ayisha told me about the constant tension she had with her sisters and an anger that overwhelmed her much of the time. They argued about everything. She wanted peace in her family and freedom from these feelings. I knew how she could find freedom! Leaning forward with the adrenaline of a great idea, I asked her to read the Bible with me, to find the peace she sought.

"Satan, the current prince of this world, has a plan for your life. He wants to destroy you and lie to you that you can never be free from this anger you feel toward your sisters. He wants you to believe that your relationships with them could never get better. But it isn't true. The only way you can be free and for your relationships with your sisters to be truly healed is for *you* to change. God can help you if you follow his ways, which are life-giving and true. And we can know his ways if we read the Bible together," I said.

I didn't want her to confuse religious labels with my offer to read the Bible for answers, so I drew a circle on a napkin.

"This circle is the kingdom of God, where the will of heaven happens. This is the only place you can be truly free. Listen: you know me well enough that you know we're not going to talk about religion. That's not what this is about. It's about learning to walk fully submitted to the will of God by following Jesus the Messiah. You remember, he is the straight path into this kingdom and the appointed King of the kingdom. What he says goes, because that's how God set it up. And his ways really work in our lives when we do what he says."

I paused to let it sink in, sensing the presence of the Spirit in that moment. "So, God meant for life to be full of his peace. If you want it, then let's start meeting together specifically to read the Bible. You'll learn how to handle anger and find answers to resolve the relationship with your sisters."

I invited her into an intentional, specific discipleship relationship with me, as we pursued the possibility of a discipleship relationship with Jesus.

"Okay, let me think about it," she replied.

"You can either go on with this terrible anger and these awful, tension-filled nights with your sisters, or you can try something else to be free," I urged.

"Yes. Let's do it. I agree. I want to read with you."

After that, we met every couple of weeks at the same vintage coffee shop, with beaded lamps and secondhand couches. I remember the spiced chai tea we ordered each time, frothed in a crock mug, and how we always split one huge piece of homemade carrot cake. We studied the Bible, yes, but we also shared our lives in between the times we met. As we tried to understand and obey the scriptures we read, it bled into the fabric of our daily lives.

She started to obey Jesus in regard to her sisters. She practiced honoring them above herself, loving them in practical ways, overlooking their offenses, and forgiving them. She began to pray blessings on them, which lessened her desire for revenge and gave her self-control. Released from Ayisha's disapproval and attempts to control, her sisters softened, and their relationship dramatically improved. She tasted the ways of Jesus and found them appealing.

Bringing Jesus into our cross-cultural relationships and deepening the level of our conversations doesn't have to be difficult, uncomfortable, or scary, as we might think. Too often we forget we already have everything we need to do this. In Jesus' last words to his disciples, when he sent them into the world, he reminded them of his authority over everything and his promise to be with them as they did his work. What is that work he gave them his authority and presence to do?

> Therefore [because I have all authority], go and make disciples of all the nations [the *ethne*, the people groups], baptizing them in the name of the Father and the Son and the Holy Spirit. Teach these new disciples to obey all the commands I have given you. And be sure of this, I am with you always, even to the end of the age. (Matt. 28:18–20)

Make disciples. And with the authority and presence of Jesus himself, we can do it. Take heart! Have courage!

What Is Discipleship, Anyway?

The word *discipleship*, the process of teaching disciples to obey all the commands of Jesus, is thrown around fairly casually in Western Christianity. But what exactly is discipleship? How do you *do* it? Is it discipleship if you lead a Bible study at church? Is it one-on-one accountability meetings? Is it encouraging people to attend church, worship, and read their Bibles regularly?

The product of your discipleship efforts will show you the effectiveness of your discipleship process. And the product of discipleship efforts are, of course, disciples.

THE PRODUCT OF YOUR DISCIPLESHIP EFFORTS WILL SHOW YOU THE EFFECTIVENESS OF YOUR DISCIPLESHIP PROCESS.

But what is a disciple, exactly? A disciple is a follower. A disciple follows someone and aspires to be like that person. That's why Jesus called the twelve friends who followed him everywhere his disciples. Buddha had disciples. Confucius had disciples. Matt, my neighbor next door, who is a jiujitsu coach, has disciples. People come to him for learning. They want to be like him and fully devote themselves to do what their master does in his area of expertise.

Making disciples—or discipleship—is the process in which you invite a person (or more than one person) to participate in your life, encouraging that person to do what you do. All of us who profess to follow Jesus are disciples of Jesus. In the Gospels Jesus invited specific people into intentional discipleship relationships with him. He called out to them, "Come, follow me, and I will show you how to fish for people!" (Matt. 4:19). He loved them, modeled service and obedience, asked questions, and provided experiences until his disciples learned what he wanted them to learn. He even sent his disciples out on practice runs on their own, telling them, "Go and announce to them that the Kingdom of Heaven is near. Heal the sick, raise the dead, cure those with leprosy, and cast out demons. Give as freely as you have received!" (Matt. 10:7–8). He knew they were catching it when they did what he did. Eventually, they grew into people who spoke and acted more like Christ, and the people around them did too. This is our goal as we seek to deepen our cross-cultural friendships into discipleship relationships.

Scripture as Our Primary Discipleship Tool

God gave us the Bible as our guidebook for teaching our disciples to follow him. When a young couple named Christopher and Sara asked a seasoned discipler, Robert, how to make disciples, he said, "You could ask most of the people you already know just to read the Bible with you. Your non-believing friends, as well as believers."

"Okay," they said. "But how?" They wondered how to go from praying occasionally with someone, serving that individual in specific ways, and telling an occasional Jesus story—to studying the Bible regularly together in a discipleship relationship.

"Just ask them to read with you," said Robert. Could it be that easy? Yes! We can do this too. When we sense spiritual receptivity in someone, we can simply ask, "Have you ever read the Bible? Would you like to read it with me?" The Bible is the Word of God. It is the primary textbook, with the Holy Spirit as teacher, to guide our friends to live the life God intended for them to live. We can invite someone to read the Bible with us far sooner than we usually think is appropriate, thus inviting him or her into a discipleship relationship with us.

Christopher and Sara decided to try it. They wrote down all the names of people they knew and started asking them to read the Bible with them.

Christopher and the Sikh Engineer

Christopher asked a Sikh engineer named Raj at his workplace, "Have you ever read the Bible? Would you like to read it with me sometime?" (As Westerners, we agonize about being so direct about spiritual matters. But people from non-Western cultures often think it's as normal to talk about spiritual topics as it is for us to discuss sports and the weather.)

Raj replied, "I haven't. No one ever asked me. Sure. Why not?"

They agreed to meet the next day over lunch and read out of Deuteronomy together:

> Listen, O Israel! The LORD is our God, the LORD alone. And you must love the LORD your God with all your heart, all your soul, and all your strength. And you must commit yourselves wholeheartedly to these commands that I am giving you today. Repeat them again and again to your children. Talk about them when you are at home and when you are on the road, when you are going to bed and when you are getting up. (Deut. 6:4–7)

Christopher followed up by asking four simple questions:

- What does this tell us about God?
- What does this tell us about humanity?
- How can we obey this?
- Who can we share it with?

At the end of a good discussion, Christopher said he planned to ask his children over dinner how they experienced God that day and share his own experience. Raj thought he should look up the commands God was referring to in the passage, so he would know what exactly he should "commit himself to wholeheartedly."

Then Christopher asked, "Would you like to do this again? If so, when is a good time?" Raj felt energized by the conversation and recognized wisdom in the passage. Curious to do more studying on his own of something that seemed to promise to make his life better, he also didn't sense any condemnation of his own beliefs.

"Sure," he said, "I'd like that. I'm free for lunch on Monday."

Christopher added, "I'm also going to tell my wife what we talked about today. She'll think it's interesting. Anybody that you could pass this on to as well? Is there anyone you know that might want to join us Monday?"[1]

Sara and Her Christian Neighbor

Sara chose to ask a believing friend, a neighbor originally from South Korea whom she saw every once in a while, to read the Word with her. She called her neighbor, Soo-min, and said, "Hey, I'm learning how to read the Bible with people in a discipleship way. Can I practice on you? Would you like to read with me once and see how it goes?"

Her friend said, "Yes, that would be great." (If you're not quite sure people will answer this easily, shed any extra agenda you have for them other than reading the Bible and doing what it says. Then just ask and see what happens!)

They found a time and place to meet: at the park with their young children the next morning. Sara selected one verse to illustrate the command for believers to make disciples who make disciples. They read what Paul wrote to Timothy:

You have heard me teach things that have been confirmed by many reliable witnesses. Now teach these truths to other trustworthy people who will be able to pass them on to others. (2 Tim. 2:2)

Sara said, "Let's look at how many layers of teaching are going on at the same time."

Outlining the passage together, they discovered three layers of discipling:

1. Paul discipled Timothy.
2. Timothy discipled other faithful men.
3. The other faithful men discipled other faithful men.

Sara and Soo-min noticed neither of them was involved in a multilayered discipleship opportunity, let alone one layer. Sara suggested they both start reading the Bible with someone else, teaching that person to read with another person, and then seeing what might happen. They searched for *Discovery Bible Study* on the internet and found lists of passages to follow.[2]

TIPS FOR READING THE BIBLE WITH CROSS-CULTURAL FRIENDS

- Find a Bible in your friends' first, heart language, and study both their language and English together.
- Allow a pause after you speak. Many people will not talk over someone else and prefer to hear a silent pause before they begin speaking. They might also need more time to formulate words about abstract concepts.
- Be respectful of the Bible. Keep it off the floor and avoid

writing in it, as this might be offensive to people from some faiths.

- Spend time talking about other things important to your friend too. Relationship is just as important as reading the Bible together.
- Teach them how to find answers to questions on their own. If you don't know the answer, discover it together in the Bible.
- Speak more slowly. Speaking slower is better than speaking louder if they don't understand you.[3]

Five Principles to Disciple People Well

If Raj and Soo-min decide to continue letting Christopher and Sara disciple them by reading the Bible, their meetings could end up as just a knowledge dump of facts. But it doesn't have to be that way. Since we're conditioned by the way we learn in school to acquire facts, we tend to see "making disciples" as simply transferring knowledge, and usually to someone who is already a believer. So, as we invite people to become our disciples, it's helpful to recognize a few mind-shifting principles about disciple making that are especially useful when we cross cultures.

#1: Disciple people into faith in Jesus Christ.

Jesus invited those who were curious, seeking God, and interested in knowing more to come and hang out with him for a while. He didn't always call them to full commitment immediately.

In Western Christianity, a popular view assumes that making disciples only occurs after someone is "saved," "born again," or "makes a decision to follow Jesus." A person comes forward at an altar call/invitation, and then great care (rightly so) is given to make sure someone follows up with them, teaching that individual how to live out his or her new faith. But this can happen the other way around also—discipleship first, and then a crossing over into new life.

We see this in the Bible when several men overheard John the Baptist say about Jesus, "Look, the Lamb of God!" Those few curious men trailed Jesus.

When Jesus noticed them, he asked what they wanted.

"Oh . . . well," they stuttered, caught off guard, "we just want to know where you're staying."

Jesus knew they weren't quite ready to consider following him yet, so he said, "Come and see!" (John 1:35–39), and they stayed with him the rest of the day.

In the same way, let's offer our friends an invitation to get to know Jesus without requiring them to fully understand the cross and all of its implications yet. When we invite them to read the Bible with us, we're simply saying, "Come and see."

#2: Stay spiritually intentional.

Only the Holy Spirit can give people new life. But we can do specific things to foster opportunity for spiritual conversations and action, if we're conscious of doing them. When I used to visit my refugee friends, sometimes I would get so busy having fun, I'd neglect to notice spiritual opportunities to go deeper. So, I made a list of questions to help me stay focused on encouraging my cross-cultural friends to consider and follow Jesus. I find that these commonsense spiritual activities often occur in this order, and some activities repeat many times. This progression can apply to *any* friendship—for those who follow Jesus and those who do not . . . yet.

Take a minute to think of a few key relationships in your life right now. Ask yourself these questions, checking off the activities you've done with these friends. When you're finished, look at the empty checkboxes. Pray and ask God what he might want you to do as a next step with each friend.

☐ Have I prayed a blessing over their home and family?

☐ Have I mentioned the name of Jesus and established in a natural way that I'm a spiritual person?

☐ Have I told a story of Jesus or the Bible in relation to something happening in everyday life?

☐ Have I prayed with them about an immediate need, asking in the name of Jesus Christ?

☐ Have I shared scripture from my daily time with God that might be encouraging?

☐ Do I know where they are hurting most or feeling lost?

☐ Do I know what things from their past need to be addressed to remove barriers to God—"rocks" that lie on their path that prevent them from being able to trust God?

☐ Have I helped them get access to the Bible in their own language, in a version that is easy for them to understand?

☐ Have I invited them and their family to read the Bible with me?

☐ Have I encouraged them to obey the scripture that we are reading together?

☐ Have I encouraged them to share with others the scripture that we are reading together?

☐ Have I praised evidence of change in their lives and hearts and in those of their family?

☐ Do I ask about evidence of change in the lives and hearts of those they are sharing with?

☐ Have I encouraged them to meet on their own to study and obey scripture as a community?

☐ Am I coaching them as they start to take responsibility for other people's spiritual growth?

#3: Do life together in a real way.

Our non-believing friends are real people with real hurts, joys, and disappointments, and we need to have real friendships with them in real life. In the West, the process of discipleship is often fairly structured and compartmentalized. We might arrange to meet once a week, sitting across a table to talk about struggles, hold someone accountable to set goals, study scripture together, and pray.

In non-Western cultures, discipleship happens in a less structured, more integrated way, talking with someone and then talking with that friend again when you see them next. A discipler might ask how his disciple practiced a recent scripture during a ride across town to help deliver goods for their business, for example. As they drink their evening chai tea in the men's tea shop after work, they might review a Bible passage verbally late into the night—as men come and go and interruptions abound. Or they might only get halfway through a discussion, and then finish another day.

Try this integrated life-on-life approach with your friends, especially those from an Eastern culture, looking for ways to do life with them. After all, this is how Jesus discipled his twelve—as they went, as they ministered, and as they lived life together. But even as we relax a little, let's keep point 2 in mind: *stay spiritually intentional.* Jesus remembered to relate everything in life to the kingdom of God in a genuine way. It's easy to forget when we aren't focused on it.

#4: Teach them to put into practice everything Jesus taught.

This element of obedience cannot be underestimated. When Jesus told his disciples to go into all the world and make disciples, he said,

"Teach these new disciples to obey all the commands I have given you" (Matt. 28:20). We must encourage our friends to put into practice what they learn and what they read in the Bible, because Jesus also said, "If you love me, obey my commandments." (John 14:15).

Often, the transforming power of the Holy Spirit makes each of our disciples a new creation in an observable way over time through their obedience. Jesus said, "You can identify them by their fruit, that is by the way they act. Can you pick grapes from thornbushes, or figs from thistles?" (Matt. 7:16). Danny, a field-worker living overseas, discipled his local friend Adam for six months before Adam came to full faith in Jesus. Earlier, Danny had prayed on the merit of Jesus Christ for Adam's unborn baby during his wife's significant bleeding. When the baby was delivered healthy, Adam and his wife attributed the miracle to the healing power of this Jesus Christ. Adam and his wife felt they should learn more about this man who had such power from God to heal, and they agreed to study the Bible together.

Danny said that he knew Adam had transferred from "come and see" to "come and follow" about six months later when Adam started washing dishes for his wife. In that country husbands never help wives with kitchen work. It is just not done. The average male stooping to such work would suffer humiliation and loss of honor. When Danny and Adam read, "Husbands, love your wives, just as Christ loved the church and gave himself up for her . . . (Eph. 5:25), they discussed specifically how and when they could love their wives in this way. Adam decided to do dishes for his wife the entire week, much to his wife's surprise and delight, because she had accidentally hurt her hand.

But let's back up a bit. How did Danny encourage Adam to *actually obey* what they were reading? As Western Christians, we don't generally expect immediate action, or obedience, to be the fruit of a church service on Sunday, or a small-group time during the week. If we do think to try and obey, we tend to be too literal, or too vague.

"Love your neighbor as yourself," said Jesus, illustrating it with the story of the good Samaritan (Luke 10:25–37). We do a quick check to remember how many beaten-up men by the side of the road we've loaded on our donkeys lately. Nope. So, we might simply scan the highway for homeless people on the way home from church to buy them a hamburger and call it good. Obedience to Jesus' commands, however, is so much more.

I read where Jesus taught that his disciples will do more miraculous things than he did, in his name (John 14:12). I looked up all the phrases with a verb that Jesus actually did and found I wasn't doing anything close to these things . . . and most certainly nothing greater. I hadn't cast out any demons lately, raised anybody from the dead, or seen any lame people walk in the last week . . . or in my whole life! I began to ask the Holy Spirit to help me believe Jesus' words and to believe them enough to *do* them in his name, because teaching others to do what Jesus taught starts with us first doing what Jesus taught.

Also, since we're obeying Jesus when he says, "Go and make disciples," if our disciples are obeying Jesus, they will be making disciples too. "Who are you sharing your learning with?" and "How are *your* disciples growing in Christ?" can be regular questions that every discipler asks. This gets left out of the discipleship process almost universally for new disciplers. If we make it an exciting expectation for our disciples to start mentoring their own disciples, it keeps the flow of disciples making disciples rapidly multiplying.

#5: Encourage discovery, rather than telling them everything you know.

All over the world, students learn in classroom settings. The teacher tells the student what to learn. The student learns the information presented, gets graded on the acquisition of that knowledge, and hopefully applies it in his or her life.[4]

In the Christian world also, pastors preach from the stage, delivering information to the "students" in the congregation and hoping they will choose to apply the information in their everyday lives. Most churches now recognize the value of self-discovery, discussion, and accountability in the learning process, encouraging their members to form midweek, smaller groups that meet in homes. These midweek small groups are more like what a new "church" of believers from non-Christian backgrounds might be like overseas. They are referred to as "house churches," "fellowships," "home groups," or such creative names as "Jesus communities," as field-workers might call them.[5]

These groups use a discovery approach to scripture, buoyed by a coaching structure, which allows everyone to hear from God through the Holy Spirit directly from the Bible. Groups learn to obey God without the baggage of foreign culture by discovering it for themselves.

You'll notice that as Christopher and Sara read together with Raj and Soo-min, they took the role of facilitator-teacher instead of lecturer-teacher, asking questions about the Bible passage. They let their friends discover the truth from the Bible themselves, rather than telling them. Together, they came up with ways to practice or obey something from the text and determined to share it with someone else. It's a healthy, communal way of pursuing character development, transformation, and Christlikeness.

Discovery processes are also easily reproducible and require neither funding nor the formal training of a learned teacher. Raj and Soo-min probably already have an extended network of family and friends in their same culture. If they learn to discover truth to follow in scripture themselves, they can easily start doing the same thing within their own cultural networks. Raj and Soo-min will be even more effective yeast in their networks and culture than Christopher or Sara could be.

Making Disciples of the Whole Family

As individualistic Westerners we sometimes forget that the gospel is for the whole family. God made families. He wants them together, and we can honor that design by including the whole family in our disciple-making process. In most non-Western cultures, families—and even entire communities, tribes, or clans—make decisions together. Rarely does a young person determine his own career path, his marriage partner, or his religious beliefs on his own. Since Westerners value independence and individual decision-making so highly, we can unintentionally rip families apart in our zeal to disciple one person at a time without regard to his or her family.

Finn, a Westerner who works in South Asia, living with unreached Muslim people groups, understands the strategic and biblical importance of family and went to great lengths to honor it. He knows the local language well and holds a solid reputation within the city as a businessman. The community regards him as a spiritual and respectful person who follows Jesus and honors God. One day, Malik, a young man from one of these unreached people groups, came to visit Finn and his wife. Malik told of how Jesus had appeared to him in a dream, and he asked Finn to teach him more about Jesus.

Finn responded, "I would love to do that. Go home and ask permission from your father, and we will discover more about Jesus together, in your home."

The color drained out of the young man's face. He drew his finger under his neck, slitting his own throat, shaking his head. His father, a Muslim sheikh (an Islamic spiritual leader), would never agree. He was right. His father refused to let him study. Finn encouraged Malik to pray and continue to ask his father's permission, honoring his father in this way.

Six times Malik came to ask Finn to disciple him, but Finn refused, instead giving him more ways to speak to his father about his interest. The young man kept telling his father how the Qur'an spoke of Jesus the Messiah more than it did any other prophet, and that his holy book actually encouraged Muslims to read the *Injil*, the Bible in Arabic.

One day, miraculously, Malik's father finally agreed. Finn began visiting the young man's home to read the Bible with him in a way that promoted discovery, encouraged obedience to the Word, and inspired sharing it with others.

Malik came to a vibrant faith in Jesus Christ, transformed by the Spirit from the inside out. Most members of his extended family also surrendered their lives to Jesus Christ, as they walked alongside him in his discipleship process. Even though his father did not (yet) embrace Jesus as the Messiah, the sheikh supported, encouraged, and blessed his son to obey and follow Christ.

The father even witnessed his son's baptism, done in his home without Finn or other Westerners present and born out of the young man's desire to obey after reading about baptism in the gospel of John. Malik became a conduit of the gospel to many others, starting Jesus communities that are multiplying rapidly, with Finn continuing to coach him.

Finn could have agreed to disciple this young man in secret, without his father's permission. It's likely Malik would have still come to faith. But his family would have been excluded, creating barriers to sharing his new faith in Jesus with them. If the local community had discovered his allegiance to Jesus Christ without going on his journey of discovery with him, they would likely have excommunicated Malik, with much shame brought on the family. In countries that operate under sharia law, a strict Islamic code, he might have even been killed.

We also can honor the family as Finn did by helping our disciples speak of their desire to learn more about God in bridging ways with their families. We can encourage them to honor their fathers and mothers when they share what they are learning as they are learning it. For international students here without their family members, we can regularly ask, "What does your father think of this passage? When could you share this with your brothers?" and remind them to thank their parents for raising them to be spiritual seekers after God.

Jesus the Messiah is for the whole family and the whole community, and we can honor the family structure when we invite people to consider Jesus Christ and the kingdom of God.

Reflection

1. What would keep you from asking non-believing and believing friends to read the Bible with you? How can you overcome those barriers and try to ask someone?
2. Which principles of discipleship are new for you, and how will you try them out with some of your friends?
3. With one cross-cultural friend in mind, complete the checklist on [page ??]. Looking at the first blank checkbox, decide how you will do that activity with your friend the next time you see him or her.

FIVE

Offering Jesus in a Winsome Way to Other Cultures

Yusef, a well-known Muslim leader from the Middle East, bowed his knee to Jesus Christ after a year of studying and putting scripture into practice when one day he announced, "I'm ready now to be fully submitted to God's will. I wish to follow Jesus the Messiah. What should I do?"

"Let's ask God," longtime field workers James and Donnah said, and prayed, "God, you are the only One who can draw someone to you. Yusef wants to be fully submitted to you. How will you show him that he can come fully under your reign and rule, through Jesus the Messiah?"

Yusef slipped to his knees on his own accord, in a half-standing, half-kneeling posture, his arms and open eyes raised to the heavens, and waited.

After some time, he stood up and said, "Jesus came and painted his blood over the door of my household. You remember how Moses and the Israelites brushed the blood of a lamb over the doorpost of their house in Egypt so that the angel of death would pass over their home. Jesus did this for us. My whole family, our entire household, all of our shame is covered by the blood of Jesus the Christ, the true anointed one of God. We are under his protection, his authority, and his guidance, and we are now citizens of his kingdom, by the will of God."

The Spirit of God had drawn Yusef to him and given him new life, which also affected his whole family. But James and Donnah also had a lot to do with the process. They'd learned to offer Jesus Christ in an attractive way. This can be challenging for Westerners when they're interacting with people from different backgrounds. Often, the struggle lies in learning how to separate the cultural parts of our personal faith, as well as our Western worldview, from the biblical parts, while also bridging current and historical perceptions of Christianity. But like Yusef's experience, it doesn't have to be complicated if we keep things free of cultural expectations, focus on Jesus, and use the kind of language Jesus used. Let's look at several winsome ways James and Donnah offered Jesus to Yusef.

Keeping the Message Pure

A while back there was a humorous commercial illustrating the static that can cloud communication in important situations. A German radio operator on a ship intercepted a call for help from a British convoy in trouble. He asked, "What is the problem?" and the British answered, "We're sinking!" The German paused, then replied, "What are you sinking about?" This is exactly the confusion we would hope to avoid when we're sharing about Jesus with our friends. So, with a critical message to deliver, we must do everything possible to make sure our message gets heard and translated correctly. James and Donnah did this in several ways.

First, they offered Jesus in a way that enabled Yusef to truly see Jesus, instead of seeing only the Western culture, or Western religious practices, that Jesus is often wrapped in. When Westerners cross cultures with the gospel, it can be difficult to keep the message free from cultural influence. Often, Christians offer Jesus *plus* . . . something else from their cultural expression of faith. A guitar for worship. A white steeple on a church building. A cross symbol. With Yusef, no guitar was ever introduced, because Muslims worship God by singing poetry acapella over a loudspeaker. There was no white steeple, or even a church building, because James and Donnah met with him in his home, surrounded by his extended family and friends. There were no crosses to be seen, because Muslims liken a cross symbol to the Crusades, when Christians marched across the land to coerce conversion with a sword. Interestingly, for the first few years after Jesus lived, his followers used the symbol of a shepherd's crook, not a cross, to represent Jesus as their Good Shepherd (see John 10:11).

> THE STRUGGLE LIES IN LEARNING HOW TO SEPARATE THE CULTURAL PARTS OF OUR PERSONAL FAITH, AS WELL AS OUR WESTERN WORLDVIEW, FROM THE BIBLICAL PARTS.

When we fail to recognize that some of our spiritual "requirements," practices, or worship styles are extrabiblical, we unwittingly pass our cultural forms on to new followers of Jesus as requirements of the faith. For example, I witnessed a prominent Indian evangelist trained in Western methods do a public baptism service for the students at his Bible school. The young men entered the waters with Hindu names, such as Prasanth or Raju. As they came out of the water, they were surprised with new names, like William Carey and John

Mark. Their new names came with complete sets of neatly pressed Western-style pants, dress shirts, and shiny black shoes—plus a host of extrabiblical practices from the evangelist's own cultural background.

Or, another example might be how we teach people to pray. Prayer often reveals cultural worship expectations. Should James and Donnah have asked Yusef to close his eyes and bow his head to pray? In what physical ways did people in biblical times pray? The Bible describes various physical postures: hands open and lifted, looking up to the sky, head covered (women), bowing down in prostration, or kneeling (Ps. 95:6; Matt. 14:19; 1 Cor. 11:5; 1 Tim. 2:8). But in nondenominational churches in the West, we fold our hands, close our eyes, keep our heads uncovered, and rarely kneel or bow. Not wrong necessarily. It's just cultural. Paradoxically, if you walk into a mosque anywhere in the world, you'll see Muslims practicing outward styles of prayer, more like the postures found in the Bible: bowing, hands lifted, or kneeling with their foreheads to the ground (Ex. 34:8; Matt. 26:39; 1 Tim. 2:8). While the Bible mentions various prayer postures, it doesn't necessarily command us to only pray in any specific physical way. So there's no need to expect—or teach—other believers from other cultures to pray the way we're accustomed to praying.

Jesus Christ is adaptable and compatible with all cultures. As we follow him into another culture, we would be wise to only bring Jesus in with us, and leave our cultural spiritual expectations at home. E. Stanley Jones, who presented Jesus to the high caste of India in the 1920s, agreed when he wrote in *Christ of the Indian Road*:

A friend of mine was talking to a Brahman gentleman when the Brahman turned to him and said, "I don't like the Christ of your creeds and the Christ of your churches." My friend quietly replied, "Then how would you like the Christ of the Indian Road?" The Brahman thought a moment, mentally picturing the Christ of the

Indian Road—he saw him dressed in Sadhus' garments, seated by the wayside with the crowds about him, healing blind men who felt their way to him, putting his hands upon the heads of poor, unclean lepers who fell at his feet, announcing the good tidings of the Kingdom to stricken folks, staggering up a lone hill with a broken heart and dying upon a wayside cross for men, but rising triumphantly and walking on that road again. He suddenly turned to the friend and earnestly said, "I could love and follow the Christ of the Indian Road."

How differs this Christ of the Indian Road from the Christ of the Galilean Road? Not at all.[1]

Second, James and Donnah offered Jesus to Yusef and his family using the language that Jesus used—talking about the kingdom of God—instead of the language of Western Christianity. Jesus spoke more than one hundred times about the kingdom of God in the Gospels.[2] We would be wise to follow his lead with our friends from other cultures. He likened the kingdom of God, where he reigns and rules as King, to the influence of yeast, the fast growth of a mustard seed, a treasure found by chance in a field, and a pearl of unparalleled value (Matthew 13). Jesus outlined and demonstrated the upside-down laws of God's kingdom, where leaders became servants (Matt. 20:25–28), evil is repaid with love (Matt. 5:43–48), and sicknesses were meant to be healed (Matt. 15:30). And what did he talk about during the forty days after his resurrection? The kingdom of God (Acts 1:3). This must be an important concept indeed!

When Yusef verbalized his surrender to Jesus, he described himself as a new member of the kingdom of God. Because Yusef had read through the Old Testament stories with James and Donnah, he knew that the garden of Eden reflected the way God's kingdom ran, where God reigned and ruled and where his will was done. God gave Adam and Eve meaningful, purposeful work with a charge to expand the garden and care for the animals so that Adam had his own kingdom to rule there, nested under God's laws.

Of course, we know that Adam rejected God's way and brought his personal kingdom outside the will of God. Ever since then, people from every country, every tribe, and every language have been trying to find a way back to God, back to the arrangement between God and man in the garden. Yusef chose to put *his* kingdom of self (where he has authority and free will to make decisions) under the authority of the kingdom of God (where God's will is done) and became part of God's kingdom (see Eph. 2:19), which the apostle Paul also described as a family (Eph. 1:5). Yusef understood that Jesus Christ made that possible through his sacrificial death and resurrection. Yusef wanted to put his kingdom of self back under the reign and rule of God by accepting Jesus' offer to make a way in, painting his blood over the door of his household, and covering his shame.

Western Christians don't often hear the gospel presented that way, do we? This realization is significant, because the traditional verbiage we use—which often goes something like "Jesus died on the cross to pay for our sins to remove our guilt so that we could go to heaven, so now you can become a Christian"—doesn't translate to Eastern cultures very well. Most Eastern cultures want their "shame" removed or their "fear" conquered, instead of their "guilt" removed, for example.[3] Also, the terms *Christian* and *Christianity* can have unfortunate meanings for many—especially for those born into faiths that are tied to cultural identity, such as Islam, Hinduism, and Buddhism. They may have deeply rooted biases because of troubled histories with those who did evil in the name of Christianity. Since most Western countries are labeled Christian in name, people from other countries think that Christians condone and live according to the immoral values the Western media portrays. They watch Western television and movies full of immodesty, immorality, and violence. They see the Kardashians wearing crosses on television—and not much else—and they think that's what it means to be a Christian.

Instead, Jesus used language such as, "The time promised by God has come at last! . . . The Kingdom of God is near [*accessible now*]! Repent of your sins [*turn from your own way*] and believe the Good News!" (Mark 1:15). This beautiful message is full of truth but free from much historical baggage and misplaced perception. So, if we can learn to discuss the basic tenets of Christianity using the language of the kingdom of God, as Jesus did, instead of language that may only speak to our culture's desires, we can offer Jesus in a more understandable way to people from other cultures and other faith traditions.

What's in a Name?

The question then becomes, how much do Yusef and his family have to give up from their cultural heritage to follow Jesus and live in the kingdom of God? Much as people in other cultures today wrestle with the implications of giving up their cultural heritage to identify as Christ followers, the early church wrestled with how much Greek believers needed to give up as they joined the faith community made up of a majority from a Jewish background (Acts 15). Did Greeks have to become Jews in order to follow Jesus? If so, circumcision would be required before they could become culturally Jewish, instead of staying culturally Greek.

The leaders in Jerusalem prayed about it and decided the answer was no. Greeks did not have to become Jews to follow Jesus. They did not need to be circumcised to show a change in their cultural heritage.

"My judgment is that we should not make it difficult for the Gentiles who are turning to God," wrote Paul (Acts 15:19).

When I first studied this, I could understand Greeks remaining Greek. However, when I replaced the word *Greek* with *Muslim*, I felt uncomfortable. After all, wasn't the designation of "Muslim" more a religious term than a cultural one? Could people retain the cultural identity aspect of being "Muslim" and still follow Jesus if they no longer followed the religion of Islam? Eventually, I realized my discomfort about this idea stemmed from an incomplete understanding of terms that, to me as a Westerner, only pointed to religion, but to people from other backgrounds, encompassed entire cultures. For most people around the world where someone is born into a religion, the terms *Muslim*, *Hindu*, and *Buddhist* are much like *American* or *Chinese* or *Canadian*. If I told my family I could no longer be American to follow Jesus, it would be absurd, and it can feel much the same way to our brothers and sisters in Christ from various Eastern cultures.

So if we seek to offer Christ to people without requiring they be stripped from their cultural families, how should we refer to them when they choose to believe? One good idea is to let them decide from their own conscience and from Scripture what to call themselves. Surprisingly, the word *Christian* only occurred three times in the New Testament. People from outside the Jewish faith used it to refer to Jews who followed Christ—and not necessarily in a nice way (Acts 11:26; 26:28; 1 Peter 4:16). Paul the apostle first referred to disciples of Jesus as "followers of the Way" (Acts 22:4). After all, the *way* is Jesus, and the *way* creates access to God. The *way* offers citizenship in the kingdom of God, through Jesus Christ, the God-appointed King of this kingdom.

As citizens of the kingdom of God, who are under the reign of King Jesus, people labeled "Christian" or "Catholic" or "Muslim" or "Buddhist" or "Hindu" can mix freely with one another as brothers and sisters in Christ without labels. Whatever term new believers adopt, though, let's help them form their identities in Christ by discovering them in the Bible. Finally, let's pray they invite their entire extended families to also give their allegiance and trust to God through Jesus Christ, as Yusef did, forming a long-lasting community for generations as they practice their faith together within the culture God gave them.

How to Make Good News Good in Other Cultures

Another challenge for Westerners offering Jesus across cultural lines is learning how to make the good news actually come across as *good*. The packaging in which we offer good news can make it attractive or leave it unopened. We don't need to feel overwhelmed or ill-equipped in this pursuit though. If we gain a few insights into how we can interact in honoring ways with people from other cultures or faiths, it will go a long way toward building bridges of peace so our message can be considered.

#1: Respect other faiths.

We must remember that we—and most people from other faith traditions and countries—have grown up believing certain things are true our whole lives. Deeply held beliefs aren't easily changed. I find that arguing, apologetics, and aggressive approaches build walls of defensiveness instead of bridges. It forces the "other side" to dig in their heels and fight back. The issue becomes being right or wrong, instead of the pursuit of godliness, righteousness, and a soft heart toward God.

At midnight one night, I stumbled across a website that detailed in a systematic, theological way the incorrect beliefs of a popular religion here in America. It seemed so logical to me that I quickly emailed the link to one of my close friends who followed this religion, thinking naively that she would say, "Wow! I never knew this. This changes everything about what I thought I believed!"

Just the opposite happened. With great courage, she asked to talk to me face-to-face. When we met, she told me, with tears in her eyes, "You deeply offended me by not respecting me, sending that link in the middle of the night as if you were just searching for something to prove I'm wrong, tearing down everything that I believe is true."

Right then and there, she helped me see how disrespectful it felt (and how awful it makes me feel) to tear down someone's beliefs. Now, when I interact with my Muslim, Hindu, and Buddhist friends, I determine never to disrespect their holy books, their prophets, or their practices. Also, if I find myself trying to win a point just to be right, I just drop it. This opens the doors of both of our hearts wide to faith conversations of much greater significance and depth.

Respect the other person's faith and practices. Find common ground and go from there. Let love, not the law, compel the conversation.

#2: Say what you mean!

The meanings of our words matter, because some words carry heavy baggage, as we discussed earlier. Some words have double meaning. Some words form a definition in one person's mind and a completely different definition in another person's mind.

> **LET LOVE, NOT THE LAW, COMPEL THE CONVERSATION.**

For example, when we say, "Jesus is the Son of God," we mean that he was born of a virgin, conceived by the power of the Spirit of God, and comes from God. In the Bible, when Mary asked how she could have a child as a virgin, Gabriel the angel answered, "The Holy Spirit will come upon you, and the power of the Most High will overshadow you. So the baby to be born will be holy and he will be called the Son of God" (Luke 1:35).

When a Muslim hears us say that Jesus is the Son of God, he or she thinks we mean that God had sexual relations with Mary and they had a child together. God forbid! On the other hand, if a Hindu hears us say that Jesus is the Son of God, since they actually do teach that some of their gods have literal wives birthing literal sons, they will assume that we believe that also. If we're not careful to say what we mean, we can do great damage to our sharing of the gospel. Casually speaking with undefined and unexplained terms such as "Son of God" because that's what we've heard in church isn't thoughtful.

This example of watching our language might raise the question of when to talk about controversial issues, like the divinity of Jesus Christ. It's interesting to observe in the Gospels that Jesus did not require his disciples to know his full identity in every aspect right from the beginning. In fact, they first regarded him as a prophet. They gradually came to see him as the Messiah with authority, and then it seems only after his death and resurrection did they attest to his divinity (Luke 24:25–43; John 20:9–10, 26–31).

Jesus let his disciples discover his full identity for themselves as they followed and experienced him. We don't need to explain all of who Jesus is right from the start. We don't even need to force new believers to recite a statement of faith on Jesus Christ's divinity right in the beginning—a complicated topic, even for scholars. Let your friends discover the truth about Jesus Christ as they discover it themselves in scripture.

#3: Expand your definition of good news.

As Western Christians we often think of the "salvation" people need most as payment for their sins so they can be with God in heaven forever. Yes, this *is* good news, and it is certainly true. But for many around the world living in pain, poverty, and persecution, for example, it doesn't address their current earthly situation. So it's not really good news to them yet.

In the Gospels Jesus didn't offer the same good news in the same way to everyone. How he offered good news always depended on the person's immediate, visible need—and his or her inner felt need. To the woman bleeding for twelve years, he offered healing . . . and emotional peace (Luke 8:48). To the despised tax collector, he offered friendship . . . and inclusion (Luke 19:10). To the child in his lap, he offered a prayer of blessing . . . and value (Matt. 19:14). To the crazy demoniac living in a cave, he offered freedom from evil spirits . . . and a right mind (Mark 5:15).

Jesus Christ *is* the good news, and his kingdom is the good news—but it comes in different packages. There are hundreds of ways in the Bible that Jesus is the good news, and we can offer Jesus in these ways to our international friends. We have the privilege to discover the customized, present way a person needs "saving" and apply the appropriate remedy. After all, a heart wound doesn't need a cast. And a broken leg doesn't need a blood transfusion.

For example, it's good news that Jesus offers his presence to homesick international students who need comfort (John 14:16–19). He offers inclusion to those refugees who feel abandoned without a country (John 15:16). He offers dignity for women caught in the slave industry who feel unworthy (Luke 7:36–50). He offers a family to orphans and widows who don't have one (Eph. 2:19). He offers provision to those living in poverty who don't have enough (Matt. 6:26). He offers exoneration to those Muslims who feel accused by religious teachers and trapped in a system of laws (John 8:1–11). He offers hope to the Hindus who feel caught in a hopeless loop of reincarnation (John 14:1–3). He offers power over evil spirits for tribal animists living in fear (Matt. 8:16). He offers justice to the oppressed minorities of the world fleeing violent regimes (Luke 4:17–21). And the list goes on and on.

#4: Be interesting: tell stories!

As we interact with our cross-cultural friends, we can tell the stories of Jesus and stories God provides in the Bible. Jesus presented most of his teaching with stories, because they illustrate principles in a more vibrant way than simply listing them out. Since many non-Western cultures are orality based, meaning they pass on their history by telling stories, they're used to speaking in stories. As you read scripture, think about how particular stories apply to everyday situations. Practice telling specific stories to yourself in a mirror or with your family, so that you really know the stories and their meanings and feel comfortable telling them well. And then trying telling one or two.

One day, I carried several bouquets of brightly colored, fresh flowers into a cinder-block refugee apartment complex. I had just read Jesus' comforting words to his disciples, "Can all your worries add a single moment to your life? And why worry about your clothing? Look at the lilies of the field and how they grow. They don't work or make their clothing, yet Solomon in all his glory was not dressed as beautifully as they are. And if God cares so wonderfully for wildflowers that are here today and thrown into the fire tomorrow, he will certainly care for you" (Matt. 6:27–30). I had practiced telling the story from this passage several times to my children, emphasizing the end, where Jesus said to "seek the Kingdom of God, above all else, and live righteously, and he will give you everything you need" (v. 33). As I did this, I was thinking of Hajer, from chapter 1, with her three small children still crammed in a tiny apartment a year after I met her. She knew very little English. She was a Muslim in a nation terrified of Muslims, carrying a deafening sense of responsibility as a single mother. Hajer needed encouragement. She didn't actually need food and clothes, but

I knew she felt worried. She needed God to encourage her to seek him and his kingdom, and then all of these other temporal, practical things would fall into their rightful place.

So I walked into Hajer's apartment, carrying those bouquets, and after kisses on cheeks and greetings, I said, "I have a story for you from the *Injil*. I think God gave it to me the other day just for you!" Other women and children in the room gathered around to hear. Those flowers and that story led to hands clinging to me in desperate hope, with tearstained faces turned toward heaven.

We prayed together for God to help them trust him first and for God to show them how he would provide for their impossible situations. The orange, yellow, and red flowers from the bouquets wore their bright clothing in Hajer's gray apartment as a reminder that if God dresses the flowers more beautifully than he dresses kings like Solomon, how much more will he care for them as they chase after God and his kingdom. And you can bet everyone in the room remembered the story and what it meant to them.

#5: Pray for people in the moment.

Just as the story with Hajer led to prayer, almost any interaction with someone can lead to prayer. We offer Jesus in a compelling way when we take every opportunity to pray to God for them in Jesus' name. I try to offer prayer the first time I meet someone from another culture by praying a blessing over their family or for something that God highlights to me in that person. In many cultures prayer is honorable and desired. It also softens hearts and allows God to interact in a way that is unique to the needs of people's souls.

After I met Ayisha and Hajer, other refugee families living in the same area folded me warmly into their circle of friendships. One woman, Maryam, asked me to pray often, for her mother, or her family, or some illness. When we pray with people, it establishes us as spiritual people right from the beginning. People are drawn to Jesus in us.

One day, Maryam called me, crying, and said, "My son was beat up on the playground today because he is Muslim! We came to America to flee war and beatings and kidnappings, and here we are, still not safe! I do not know what to do. Please, will you pray for me? God always seems to listen to you!" I prayed with her right then, over the phone, and also gave some advice about how to bring these situations to the school principal's attention.

An hour later, she called me back, elated. "God heard your prayers, even before I could talk to the principal!" She sounded incredulous. "The school called me and moved my son to another class right away. They put the other child on suspension. I feel safe now. How do you have this kind of faith? How does God always listen to you like this? I wish that I knew."

It's easy to tell someone, "I'll pray for you," and then not really pray for that hurting person. If I had not prayed for Maryam right in the moment, I would have missed out on the chance to enter into a deep heart experience with her . . . and God.

Also, we don't have to wait until someone asks us to pray. We can initiate prayer in the moment by asking, "How can I pray for you and for your family?" Prayer times are moments when God breaks through from heaven to earth, speaking into someone's life, turning his or her face toward him. These moments can also lead to something more—like friendship or healing, listening to stories, reading scripture together, or even someone walking into the kingdom of God in full faith.

In this case, I felt the Spirit prompting me to keep going with Maryam.

"Maryam, you can pray like this too. God will listen to you. He will even speak back to you to give you wisdom to know what to do."

"What?! How? Tell me right now. I want this!" she said.

"Well, it's something that must be learned over time. If you will meet with me six times, we will look at all the prophets that both you and I know. Each of them has a message, a sign from God. At the end of six weeks, you will be able to go straight to God, and he will listen to you," I suggested.

Curious now, and invested in the outcome, she agreed to this plan, creating a way for us to meet regularly to read scripture about something important to her. If our eyes are spiritually open, God will show us the ones he wants us to encourage through prayer . . . and it often leads to something more.

Let's pause and ask God to help us share good news in a way that is good news for others.

Father God, I want to share good news, so others can receive it like a beautiful gift. Please help me to do as Paul wrote in 2 Corinthians 2:14 and "spread the knowledge of Christ every-where, like a sweet perfume." Give me the patience to build bridges with people from other cultures and faiths and not try to merely win arguments. Keep my words understandable, and make me conscious of how others might perceive the terms I use. Give me insight into the hurting and lost places inside of people, so you can fill those places with healing and hope. Help me to see beyond people's words and actions and discern what is really keeping them from believing God. Keep my speech fresh with new stories I'm reading from your Word every day, and give me insight to notice when I could pray with someone right in the moment.

Reflection

1. What cultural practices do you need to shed from your concept of Western Christianity in order to build bridges and offer Jesus Christ in a winsome way?
2. How would you explain the gospel using kingdom-of-God language? What is new about that idea for you?
3. Write down the names of the people from other cultures that you know. Put a plus sign next to those you know are true followers of Jesus. Put an empty checkbox next to those you know are not true followers of Jesus. Put a question mark next to those you don't know about.
4. For the + people, when you see them next, talk with them about how their cultural identity meshes with their spiritual identity. Share some of your new learning about offering Jesus in a winsome way. For the empty boxes, think about the ways they might feel lost, and how Jesus is the good news in specific areas. For the ? people, this may show that you haven't had enough spiritual conversations with them. Determine to tell a story or pray for something in their lives with them.

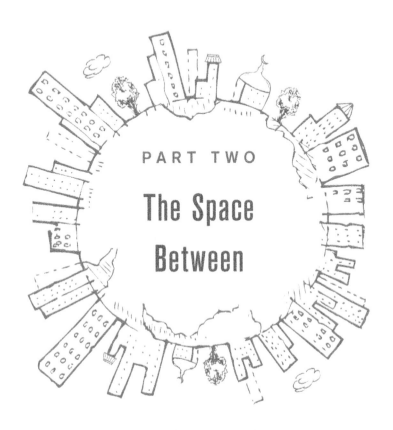

PART TWO

The Space Between

Building a Bridge
Between "Here"
and "There"

SIX

Increasing Your Missional Intelligence (MQ)

We were a sight to behold. Twenty-two wide-eyed Americans crammed into one nine-person van in the middle of India. Dodging cows and people, the driver followed a dump truck piled high with our forty-four duffel bags, veering sharply every now and then in games of chicken with oncoming vehicles. Beanie Babies, stuffed animals, filled twenty-two of the forty-four bags, gifts we hoped would make two thousand orphan children smile. Indeed, when we finally arrived and proudly handed out our gifts, everyone did smile. And stare. With bewilderment. It seemed to them an odd and impractical gift for children without shoes or enough food to eat.

For two weeks, the local Christian leaders who ran the orphanage paraded us in front of meetings and awards assemblies, with heavy flowers garlanding our necks as we listened to long speeches. We stood in lines to distribute candies and stuffed animals to children being herded into order with sticks and snapping rags. We spoke at their Bible training school, where no one understood our English. And after doggedly pushing a project to photograph, medically assess, and document all the orphans in a database—a project they didn't ask for—we left. We felt confused, depressed, and disappointed, not at all sure why we felt so awful.

After all, we'd had the best of intentions in going to India. No matter that none of us had bothered to take any pre-trip training or that most of the group had never been outside of the United States before. After the trip, we shrugged off our uneasiness, raised half a million dollars for the organization, and hoped everything would turn out okay.

When I returned a year later, the stuffed animals we'd given lined the private room of one of the adult caretakers, and the rest had been sold or stolen. The staff no longer used the medical database because the person who knew how to use it had left, and the computers stopped working in the humidity and heat anyway. Plus, the children came and went frequently, and with a ratio of one adult to fifty children, the staff couldn't keep track.

It also turned out the Bible school that trained men and women to go to north India with the gospel couldn't find the chronological Bible teaching set we had given them. On top of that, jealous over the generous flow of Western money pouring in, the fundamentalist Hindu-majority city officials accused the well-regarded school director of running a prostitution center for white men. The director spent forty nights in jail on charges that were later dropped.

As the trip leader and main champion in the West for the cause of these underprivileged children and people without access to Jesus Christ in India, I felt responsible. A friend, seasoned with years of global experience, observed that none of us connected with championing and funding this global cause had much missional intelligence quotient, a new term I'm calling MQ.

He asked, "Besides the fact that you know nothing about child development, poverty alleviation, and community development, do you know what people group these children come from? Are they unreached or unengaged? Hindu, Muslim, Sikh, Jain, or Buddhist?"

My thoughts raced. *People group? What's that? Unreached? Unengaged? What does that mean? Why is it important that I know whether they're Hindu, Muslim, Buddhist, or . . . What are Sikhs and Jains?!*

He advised I get some training to increase my MQ so that I could be more strategic and effective, putting my zeal to better use.

I listened, and I did it.

In the fifteen years since that trip, with increased MQ, more experience, and more observation in my back pocket, I now understand the importance of feeding our minds as much as we feed our souls and our hearts. When it comes to engaging with the world in a helpful way, we need to eagerly and constantly upgrade our learning while we continue to act, with humility. Passion without knowledge is dangerous.

PASSION WITHOUT KNOWLEDGE IS DANGEROUS.

Do we know what we don't know? So many of us let global things be done without appropriate learning first. Activist Martin Luther King Jr. said, "Nothing in all the world is more dangerous than sincere ignorance and conscientious stupidity," and the same rings true in our global strategies for advancing God's kingdom.[1]

Adopting the Posture of a Learner

Missional Intelligence Quotient (MQ) is not *just* about acquiring knowledge. It's about developing the continuing posture of an eager learner, so that we can be spiritually strategic while we take action. Before we grow our MQs with some basics, let's understand the attitude we must adopt to more intentionally engage with the nations—one of humility, thoughtfulness, and commitment to learning.

It's a tragedy that Christians often approach decisions regarding global work without the same level of intention and thought given to other decisions of significance. For example, when our high school senior considered which university to attend, we prayerfully sought the Lord about her calling and God's will for her life. She also took career and personality tests, searched through endless degree options, and visited universities while making a list of pros and cons. We considered finances, friends, school reputation, and the potential return on investment for her future. In contrast, when it comes to missions, well-meaning Christians sometimes imply it's almost unspiritual to employ strategy and logic to advance God's kingdom.

But Jesus said, "And you must love the LORD your God with all your heart [*passion*], all your soul [*will*], all your mind [*intelligence*], and all your strength [*effort*]" (Mark 12:30). God wants us to use our intelligent minds as much as he wants to use our passions, efforts, and will to persevere. Let's consider the big-picture strategy before we make quick decisions or walk into situations that could end up being ineffective or, worse, hurt those we're trying to help. It is not unspiritual to combine strategy with the guidance of the Holy Spirit, especially considering how complex cross-cultural work can be.

When I first visited India with that team of twenty-two, I underestimated the complexity of the world. I underestimated the complexity of other cultures and of deeply held belief systems. I didn't understand the root causes for disturbing issues such as poverty, slavery, and war—and their corresponding solutions. I didn't learn what I needed to know ahead of time, and because of that, our efforts proved less than helpful.

Sometimes this mind-set happens because we don't hear about certain topics in our church services, or even our missions weekends—topics like effective community development, asset-based poverty alleviation strategies, and how and when to turn relief efforts into a rebuilding phase. We do rightly hear and respond to statements such as, "Give twenty-five dollars a month to help an orphan eat and go to school in Africa." Unwittingly, though, we start believing that the problem and the solution are that simple. And we start to think we know best.

The sad outcome of this is that there is sometimes an unspoken refusal in Western Christianity to learn from other cultures, from those who've gone before us, or from those who are currently working cross-culturally. Many don't appreciate history, shrugging it off as old news in the search for innovation. But without this humility to learn, we will find ourselves making the very mistakes that others made before us. It takes humility to admit that we don't know, and that we need to learn more.

Another roadblock to adopting a learner's posture is our Western desire for immediate results. Our attention spans are short. For example, there's a well-known course on the biblical, historical, strategic, cultural, and partnership frameworks for global missions, called Perspectives on the World Christian Movement. It's offered in variations all over the world. This three-hour class every week for fifteen weeks has a fee, and participants write research papers at the end.[2] Take a class or take a trip? Most Christians interested in missions would prefer to raise thousands of dollars to drink the adrenaline of yet another short-term trip instead of putting in the time to take a class first. It's the Nike syndrome of global work: just do it. All you need is a pair of great running shoes, and you can win that marathon.

I confess I had that exact mind-set at one point. But someone who cared about global work being done well dragged me into the Perspectives course one day. I sat slumped in the back with my arms folded, tapping my toes with impatience. But by the end of the first class, my own arrogance had drowned in a sea of valuable information I'd never heard before. I started listening. I had already spent ten years making mistakes as I tried to make a difference in the world before then. As my eyes began to open, I regretted waiting so long. This course reshaped the next ten years of my life, and I want the same for you.

But before we dive into some foundational learning together about the state of the world and the task left unfinished, let's take a minute right now to pray and ask God for the persistence and humility to learn what we need to *know* while we *do*.

God, please open my mind to new ideas, new information, and new sources of learning that I never knew about. Lead me to the right people and places to learn what you want me to learn as I go. I don't want to use ignorance as an excuse for executing work in other cultures poorly. I give you my pride in thinking I know it all. Please humble me and let me better appreciate the experiences, wisdom, and viewpoints that others may have to offer.

Lord, I give you my mind. I acknowledge that you gave me my intelligence, my experiences, and education and that you wish me to use them all. Help me embrace the idea that it's okay to be both strategic and spiritual, and to be strategic about spiritual things. Lord, thank you for the sense of urgency you've given me, as well as the drive to succeed, but give me patience to not go ahead of you too quickly.

The MQ Foundation: Reaching Every Nation

Just as our IQ, or our level of intellectual intelligence, correlates with how well we might be able to solve puzzles or math problems, our level of MQ, or our missional intelligence, correlates with how well we might be able to address the Matthew 28:19 mandate to go into all the world. Missional intelligence is about strategy. It's about understanding God's goal, what it means to win, and what it's going to take to get there.

God's goal all along—from the Old Testament through the New Testament—has been to invite people to return to a right relationship with him. God's primary purpose is to reconcile all people to himself. "And all of this is a gift from God, who brought us back to himself through Christ. And God has given us this task of reconciling people to him. . . . We speak for Christ when we plead, 'Come back to God!'" (2 Cor. 5:18, 20).

With God's goal of reconciliation in mind, Jesus told us what it would take to win. Every nation needs a chance to hear about and experience the kingdom of God. Jesus said, "The Good News about the Kingdom will be preached throughout the whole world, so that all nations will hear it; and then the end will come" (Matt. 24:14). And that "end" he was talking about? It's when people from all nations worship God together in the next life. The apostle John wrote, "After this I saw a vast crowd, too great to count, from every nation and tribe and people and language, standing in front of the throne and before the Lamb. They were clothed in white robes and held palm branches in their hands" (Rev. 7:9).

Now, knowing what it means to win—getting to the point where every nation is in possession of the good news of the kingdom—we need to figure out what it will take to get there. Let's increase our strategic MQ by learning what the Bible means by "nations," discovering which nations still need access to Jesus, what blocks of people belong to those nations, and how we're doing getting to those nations.

What is a nation, and why is that so important?

Why will a Hindu Brahman man never marry a Muslim woman, even if she is as wealthy and educated as he? Why do Chinatowns exist all over the world where transplant Chinese re-create the culture of their home country? If we travel to a different country, why do we brighten at the sight or sound of people who look and sound like us? Because people from different nations are different from each other, and we naturally gravitate toward the comfort of sameness.

The Greek word for nations—*ethne*—is from the same root as our English word *ethnicity*. So when we talk about the nations, we're refer-ring to large groups of people who have common racial, national, tribal, religious, linguistic, or cultural origins or backgrounds.[3] Someone with a specific ethnicity belongs to a group of people who speak the same language and have similar cultural practices. It's human nature to want to hang out with people who speak like us, look like us, and act like us.

In MQ language, these natural ethnic groupings—the nations or the *ethne*—are called *people groups*. Understanding people groups is an important part of growing our MQ, because the gospel can spread within a people group without running into walls of misunderstand-ing, but that doesn't mean the same strategy will naturally cross over into other people groups.[4] There are more than six thousand people groups—like the Kurds of Iraq—who don't have enough native Christ followers to effectively share Jesus within their groups. So the gospel can't spread without outside help. Believers from another people group (like Canadians or Americans or South Koreans) will need to cross over into the Kurdish people group to learn their language and live like them, so the Kurds can embrace the gospel for themselves. So, with elevated MQ, those who are willing to cross cultures with the gospel should focus on those six thousand people groups.

What complicates matters is that within the same country there might be several different people groups, something we in the West don't always know. If we don't have much MQ, we might lump everyone living in Iraq into one category, call them Iraqis, and not even realize the Kurds need a unique gospel effort, separate from one that focuses on the Sunni or Shia Muslims, also living in Iraq. After all, they're all Iraqi, aren't they? But in Iraq, the Kurds speak Kurdish and are completely different culturally from the Iraqi Arabs who live there. They don't intermarry. They don't have anything to do with each other. The gospel won't flow between those groups naturally.

It's important to grasp this concept of *ethne* because, as we noted earlier, Jesus said the end will come only when all the *ethne* hear about the good news of the kingdom of God. Some from all the nations of the world—including these six thousand distinct people groups—still need a chance to be reconciled to God through Jesus Christ.

What is "unreached" and "unengaged," and why is that important?

Since we now know that every people group must have a chance to hear about the kingdom of God (Matt. 24:14), we need to know which people groups are *not* getting to hear and in what nations the message of Jesus Christ is not even being offered—by anyone. This is where the terms "unreached" and "unengaged" come in. If we understand what these terms mean, we can dream about what it will take to reach those people groups with the least access to the good news.

"Unreached-ness," in MQ language, is about *access* to the gospel. While I was in India, my neighbors belonged to a Muslim people group of ten million. Out of that ten million, less than a few hundred people follow Jesus. Not enough of them know about Jesus Christ to reach the rest of the people group. Thus, they do not have access to the gospel. They are unreached.

Keep in mind that unreached is not the same as unsaved. There are families living on my street in America who are not following Jesus, just like the neighbors on our street where we lived in India. However, my neighbors in the United States belong to a population in which the majority of people call themselves Christians.[5] My neighbors in America have access to the gospel. They are not saved, but neither are they unreached. A people group is generally considered unreached if the number of evangelical Christians is less than 2 percent of the population.

A second important word to increase your MQ is the concept of "unengaged" people groups. James Gilmour, field-worker to Mongolia in the 1800s, said, "I thought it reasonable that I should seek to work where the work was most abundant *and the workers fewest.*"[6] The "workers fewest" referred to people groups that were unengaged. This means there are not enough field-workers even *trying* to reach a people group. It's similar to the way Coca-Cola, though it holds one-third of the entire world's nonalcoholic beverage market, is not at all prevalent in North Korea and Cuba, the only countries that don't officially sell Coca-Cola products. Their people will never drink Coke, because it's not even being offered there. Yes, they are unreached with Coca-Cola, because not enough people have access to it, but no one is even trying to get it to them, so they are also unengaged.[7]

Here are a few examples of this being played out among actual people groups: Seventy-five million Turks are unreached because they have less than a 2 percent Christian population. They do not have access to Jesus. But thank God that twelve hundred field-workers live with the Turks. For the time being, as of 2018, they are engaged.

In contrast, six of the sixty-plus unreached Muslim people groups in the country of Chad don't have *any* field-workers trying to reach them—and they have populations of more than one hundred thousand. The Muslim people groups of Chad are unreached, and several of the large people groups still remain entirely unengaged. No one is even trying to reach them!

To add to the strategic complexity, some massive people groups, like the 150 million Bengalis, are under-engaged. A few field workers live in the north of the country, but some of the southern districts don't have people intentionally sharing Jesus Christ there. In some locations, Bengalis have less than the equivalent of half of a field-worker per million Bengalis. Do you see how increasing our MQ in strategy will help us focus our efforts where the need is greatest?

What is "movement thinking," and why is that also important for our MQ?

People with high MQ understand Jesus' principle of multiplication, or "movement thinking." When a good seed is planted in good soil, Jesus expects it to reap one hundred times over (Matt. 13:8). So, while we start with one seed or one person—and it often takes an outside person to plant that seed—we plant it in a way that it can reproduce a hundred times over.

In MQ language, this is called a disciple-making movement (DMM). This means there's not just one group of believers meeting in a home, but many, spreading like wildfire in areas of the world far away from where you and I live. It starts with one group. Then two churches become four, and four become eight and eight become sixteen. We won't hear about these thousands of new believers in the media. They spread from within a culture, without visible buildings, in an organic way reminiscent of the rapid growth in the book of Acts.

How do these movements occur—and how are they sometimes stunted? History shows that some activities stop a movement dead in its tracks. Inexperienced field-workers, short-term trip people, or well-intentioned funders can do what seem like good things, starting one or two churches, but end up stopping movements since they're not naturally replicable. We sometimes do this when we build buildings that local people couldn't or wouldn't build again on their own, extract local believers to Western Bible schools instead of teaching them to discover what faith looks like in their own contexts, and pay local evangelists instead of helping them find ways to support themselves so they're not dependent on outside funding to expand. However, we can all encourage activities to foster movements within unreached people groups when we teach broader practices that aren't rooted in one particular culture, such as organizing excessive prayer, encouraging the training of believers right where they live, and finding ways to provide scripture in the people group's heart language, the one they speak in their homes.[8]

So, who are the most unreached peoples?

Now that we understand what "people groups," "unreached," "unengaged," and "movement thinking" mean, it's strategic to discover who the people groups are that are unreached and in need of a disciple-making movement. Then we'll know where to best focus our global efforts. We'll know who to pray for, how to give, where to send short-term teams, and how to focus long-term work.

The Most Unreached Peoples (as of 2016)

Segment	Population	Percentage of the World	Unreached People Groups
Tribal Animist	206 million	2.9 percent	1,004
Hindu	1,028 billion	14.7 percent	2,314
Unreligious	1,291 billion	18.6 percent	428
Muslim	1,537 billion	22 percent	2,854
Buddhist	621 million	8.9 percent	449
Christian (as a comparison, includes all Catholic and Protestant)	2 billion	28.6 percent	0

Most of the world's unreached people groups—comprising more than 2.8 billion people—fall into one of five major categories: Tribal, Hindu, Unreligious, Muslim, and Buddhist. It's easy to recall if you remember the acronym THUMB.[9]

Take a look at both the population sizes and the number of people groups.[10] All of these are a priority, but which rises to the top based on how many are unreached today? Muslims and Hindus. These two blocks represent well over two-thirds of the remaining unreached people groups and over a third of the world's population. Where do they live? Not surprisingly, almost all Hindus live in India. You may not know, though, that only one out of every five Muslims live in the Middle East and have an Arab background. The majority of Muslims live in Asia and North Africa. According to an international sending organization focused solely on reaching Muslims, the highest concentrations of unengaged Muslim people groups are located in Indonesia, India, Bangladesh, Pakistan, Chad, Sudan, the Russian Caucasus region, and the Arab Gulf countries.[11] Also, many international students and refugees come from unreached people groups in one of these five categories, coming to live right in our own cities.

How is the church reaching out to unreached people groups?

Statistically speaking, it would be possible to impact every unreached people group for the gospel—if we only would do it. For every one unreached people group, there are nine hundred churches, as well as seventy-eight thousand evangelical Christians, in the world. The Traveling Team, an organization that gathers missions statistics, wrote, "There are 4.19 million full-time Christian workers [*this number includes pastors, and those working in university outreach and non-profits, as well as foreign field-workers*] and 95% are working within the Christian world."[12]

When the Western church does send field-workers long-term, most do not choose to go to unreached people groups. "I'm moving to Uganda . . . to South Africa . . . to Brazil . . . to Florida!" say most people who consider long-term foreign fieldwork. Of course, any effort to advance the gospel is worthy, but the truth is, choosing these better-known destinations only serves to reach the already-reached people groups who live there. For every one hundred people who decide to go to the nations long-term, seventy-three of them go to people groups that already have Christians and churches.[13] The tragedy is that evangelical Christians could be reaching people groups with little access to Jesus Christ faster—if field-workers went more strategically, with more missional intelligence.

Number of International Field Workers Going to Every Million . . .

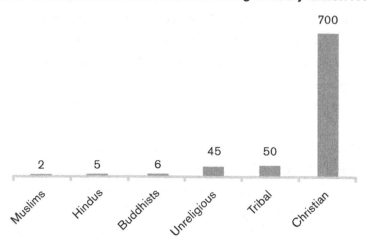

Where does the bulk of the Western church's missions giving go?

"Americans have recently spent more money buying Halloween costumes for their pets than the amount given to reach the unreached," reports the Traveling Team. Christians worldwide give one dollar for every one hundred thousand dollars they make toward reaching unreached people groups.[14]

Out of all the funds designated for "missions" in the United States, about 5 percent is used for foreign missions. Of that total, only 1 percent is used to take the gospel to unreached people groups, including refugees being resettled in Western countries. This means that only about one cent out of every one hundred dollars given to missions goes toward reaching the people with the least access to the

FOR EVERY ONE HUNDRED PEOPLE WHO DECIDE TO GO TO THE NATIONS LONG-TERM, SEVENTY-THREE OF THEM GO TO PEOPLE GROUPS THAT ALREADY HAVE CHRISTIANS AND CHURCHES.

gospel. The rest goes toward efforts to further reach already-reached people groups. While giving to reached people groups is still worthy, the drastic imbalance means that unreached people groups remain unreached.[15]

How can we then use our MQ and be strategic about unreached people groups right now?

There's actually a lot we can do right here right now. We can research, dream, and mobilize prayer for these unreached people groups. We can give financially to field workers who go live with them. We can focus our short-term efforts on getting long-term work into these groups. We can work for nonprofits that specialize in them and befriend people from unreached people groups when they enter our home countries as refugees or international students.

Some of us also might dedicate our lives to be messengers of the gospel to an unreached people group, moving to where they live and learning their language and culture. Then we may become catalysts of church planting, poverty alleviation, education, and social justice in those communities, planting the seed of the kingdom of God and launching movements to Jesus Christ.

"I'm going to the Pashtun of Afghanistan . . . the Persians in Iran . . . the unreligious in North Korea (yes, someday that country will open up and someone must be ready to go in) . . . the Sheikh Bengalis of Bangladesh!" say only a very few aspiring cross-cultural workers.

But get ready! Church leaders are ramping up on their missional intelligence. There's mounting energy as prayer, focus, and the strategic conversation grows to highlight unreached people groups to everyone. So let's focus our efforts across the street and around the world on unreached, unengaged, and under-engaged people groups. Let's chase after global learning of all kinds and equip ourselves with knowledge so that when God begins tugging at our hearts to act for the nations, the Holy Spirit has something to work with.

Take a minute now to pray and ask God to increase your MQ:

Lord, I'm overwhelmed and inspired with all these numbers and statistics. Help me to picture each number as a person—a child, a mother, a brother, a husband, or a wife. Each of these groups of people is precious to you. Give me your heart for them. Help me see them as you see them. God, stir up my heart the way yours stirs for the desire to see all people groups—all the nations—worship you. Please open my eyes to how I can get involved in your great cause to bring freedom to the nations, through Jesus Christ.

Reflection

1. Which statistics grabbed your attention the most? Pray over them, and ask God what he wants you to know about them.
   - Browse through the following practical applications for feeding your missional intelligence, your MQ. Choose one or two, and make a plan for when to do it.Sign up for the course Perspectives on the World Christian Movement (www.perspectives.org).
   - Join or start a goer missional community group, following the Small Group Plan at the end of this book.
   - Read through people group lists and profiles to find unreached people groups to fill your prayer life and capture your focus (start with https://joshuaproject. net or *Operation World: The Definitive Prayer Guide to Every Nation*, by Jason Mandryk).
   - Invite a field worker out to dinner and ask questions.
   - Read books about specific aspects of global work you're especially interested in.
   - Print maps and examine them. Study them and search for peoples and places online. Let those places fill your imagination and inform your dreams.
   - Follow international sending organizations on social media, sign up to get their resources, and attend their training opportunities.
   - Get a degree or audit university classes in an area of study related to global work.
   - Read and put into action the rest of this book.

SEVEN

Planning and Participating in Effective Short-Term Trips

After a few years working with refugees and international students and making intentional cross-cultural friendships in our city, my husband and I felt the nudge to explore what might lie beyond. Clothed with a learner's attitude and increased MQ, we landed in India for a short survey trip alongside another couple. We went, asking God a few questions: *God, what do you want us to know about reaching this unengaged, unreached people group with the gospel? What role would you have us play?*

The first night, we ate dinner in a local restaurant, in the center of the city quarter. As we tried to scoop a spicy chicken curry into our mouths, braving bold stares in a place where few other Westerners ever came, a local man sidled up to us. He asked, "Why are *you* here?" or maybe it sounded more like, "Why are you *here?*"

"Oh, we're just trying to see if the kingdom of God is already here. Do you know of it?"

"The kingdom of God?" He paused and scratched his head. "Oh, I think it is just north of here."

The next day, we did indeed catch a glimpse of the kingdom of God in a man we called Cornelius, a busy historian who agreed to talk with us about that region. Cornelius, of course, again asked us the standard question when Western people show up in a city without any Westerners in it: "Why are *you* here?"

"We are businesspeople working in companies in America. We wish to move our families here to start businesses that would create jobs in your city," we replied, as we referenced our work in health care and information technology in Fortune 500 companies.

We explained that we also worshiped the one true God and wished to encourage peace between Westerners and Muslims, as well as peace between God and people. Cornelius questioned us for over an hour. Finally, he smiled and stood up.

"I will tell you about our history. But first I should tell you that I am not just an historian; I am the secretary of the chamber of commerce." He shook our hands and announced, "I would like to personally welcome you to our city. Come speak at our chamber meeting tonight. I will introduce you, and you will tell everyone why you are here!"

That evening, the group of business leaders we met with gave us a carved, wooden boat with the word "welcome" and the name of their city printed on it. This felt like a "memorial stone moment," in the spirit of how Joshua instructed the Israelites to collect twelve stones and build an altar to God after he had dried up a path for them to cross the Jordan. It was to "serve as a sign among" them, so they would not forget (Josh. 4:6).

That welcome boat was a memorial stone, a part of God's confirmation of his calling for us to go into a new land: "I want this city for myself, and you are going to be part of that plan!"

As a result of the trip, we made the decision to move to that same city. And God-fearing Cornelius continued to promote his Western friends to his business associates, friends, and neighbors.

If someone now asks about the kingdom of God, someone in that city will say, "I've seen it. It is right here!"

Purposeful short-term trips can yield a high long-term return on investment, just as this trip did. Short trips overseas serve as a bridge between our current reality and catching a vision for how God sees the world—and how we could invest long-term in that vision. Since more than two million Americans take short-term trips every year, let's spend some time learning about three different types of short-term trips that serve this purpose.[1]

Three Types of Short-Term Trips

There are strategic reasons, strategic ways, and strategic places to take an overseas trip. By understanding that short trips fall into three main categories—vision trips, professional trips, and survey trips—and that they all have different goals and expectations, we can reduce confusion, spend money more wisely, and increase our effectiveness.

When we know the reason for our trip, and thus which of the three types of trips we're taking, we can more fully explore the how, where, and with whom questions that follow. Mislabeling a trip can lead to disappointment, cultural mistakes, and tension between those working long-term on the field and the short-term goers. It can also unnecessarily waste money, since short trips tend to cost a lot. So, let's make sure we choose our trips wisely and plan them well.

Trip Type #1: Vision Trips

Vision trips, also called *exposure* or *connection trips*, help us discover God's heart for the nations in an experiential way. As team members on a vision trip, we will get more out of the trip than we give. We enter another culture as listeners and learners instead of teachers and givers, and we meet God in new ways as we walk with him into places that seem difficult and meet people who are different. This is important to keep in mind, so we don't have outsized expectations for what we'll be accomplishing.

Remember, short-term teams cannot do in ten days what it may take ten years to do. God doesn't start movements on a short-term trip's timetable. We shouldn't expect the surrender of a few days of vacation time to reap a revival. Also, short-term teams are usually randomly assembled, missionally uneducated, and culturally untrained Westerners, composed of all ages and backgrounds. These kinds of teams cannot accomplish what seasoned overseas workers, who have learned the language and culture over many years, can accomplish.

Many people try to make short-term trips out to be more than they are meant to be, mixing vision trips with professional trips or even mistaking them for long-term missions work. This may surprise you, but vision trips are actually about you and me. Not about the people we want to reach. Most short-term trips are vision trips and are mainly designed for our own transformation. It is a short-term investment in a much longer-term goal. This knowledge releases us from the guilt of needing immediate, visible results to show our financial supporters.

Be assured that most mature believers will gladly pay for you to go on an immersion experience that will bring you closer to the heart of God. With a challenge to pursue long-term work, and a soul awakened to other cultures, you may make it your life ambition to follow Jesus for a longer time into that culture. Tell your funders you're willing to consider it.

VISION TRIPS ARE ACTUALLY ABOUT YOU AND ME. NOT ABOUT THE PEOPLE WE WANT TO REACH.

Vision Trips to People in Poverty

Short-term trips are often planned to go to materially poor communities trapped for decades in chronic poverty. To support lasting change in these kinds of communities, consider designing your short-term vision trip using *Helping Without Hurting in Short-Term Missions* by Steve Corbett and Brian Fikkert. As the authors point out, "Part of the process of a short-term trip entails recalibrating our hearts and minds, moving away from easy—but incomplete and unbiblical—assumptions about the materially poor. Learning about and acknowledging the complexity of poverty, particularly in the community where you will be visiting, is an essential part of long-term engagement in missions and poverty alleviation."[2]

Zealous but uneducated short-term Westerners can do much harm to overseas communities caught in systemic poverty. To avoid this, it's wise to connect early on with an internationally recognized nonprofit with long-term field workers from your own culture already living where you're going and doing healthy community development work.

Make it a main goal for your vision trip to learn about poverty alleviation, rather than thinking you will alleviate it on the trip. Understanding the poverty mind-set, the long road to sustainable development, and learning holistic approaches is more important than getting that fence painted or that house built.

Cautions for Vision Trips

I'd like to offer a bit of advice about common mistakes Westerners make when planning two specific kinds of entry-level vision trips: those to disaster relief areas and those planned for youth in our same country.

Most short trips planned overseas from the West to areas of disaster are actually vision trips trying to complete a service project too late after a catastrophic event, such as a tsunami, earthquake, or a flood, occurs. The belated effort can do more harm than good, because the trip happens in the development phase of the rebuilding of a community. When a community is past the worst part of the crisis, it needs to rebuild.

However, when a crew of eager, Western faces with money comes in a year after the natural disaster and promises to do everything for them, treating them as if the disaster just occurred, it derails the rebuilding. The people in these situations will appear to still be in the relief phase to untrained eyes and compassionate hearts. In reality, they are in the rehabilitation or development phase, both of which require a different set of skills and a different level of interaction with the community.

When natural disasters strike around the world, unless we are trained responders or it happens in our own country, it's wiser to quickly donate funds to reputable international aid organizations on the ground, like the Red Cross, Food for the Hungry, or World Vision, rather than plan a trip to "help" them later.

Another word of advice is for project based youth trips done in our same country. Often, church youth groups offer weeklong trips for high schoolers as a discipleship opportunity, labeled as "mission" trips and promoted as service projects to low-income areas of the United States. While they may be "missional"—meaning living "on mission" every day of your life, serving others, and speaking of Jesus—they usually aren't cross-cultural. By mislabeling in-country youth trips as "missions" trips, it gives youth the impression they've experimented with or experienced cross-cultural missions work when they haven't. A notable exception would be planning a vision trip to an area of the city where refugees live—offering after-school kids camps and English conversation classes and making cross-cultural friends.

It Takes an Intentional Trip Leader!

Successful vision trips don't happen without a competent, intentional trip leader. Do you think you might want to lead a trip in an effective and fruitful way? Here's how:

- Promote and design the trip as a learning experience. Encourage your team to try new foods, talk to new people, ask new questions, think new thoughts, and pray new prayers. Model appropriate responses to disturbing things your team notices associated with injustice, poverty, and spiritual darkness. Then follow up when you return from the trip with resources for further learning, such as books, articles, and classes.
- Prioritize discipleship, and push each participant out of his or her comfort zone just enough to help every participant grow. Build in opportunities during Bible studies and daily debriefings to use scripture to promote obedience to Jesus. Use prayer times to grapple with concerns. Speak into areas of your team members' lives as you observe and interact with them throughout the day.
- Discourage repeat-trip junkies. Instead, ask repeat trip takers to lead the next trip, practice with internationals where they live, or take a step to move overseas.
- Design short-term trips that promote long-term work and longer-term goals. Expect your team members to put into practice what they've seen and experienced when they return.
- Spread the responsibility for the success of the trip by assigning roles. For example, assign a detailed person to manage the finances, a photographer to create mobilization materials, and a pastoral person to lead devotionals and manage the team's spiritual health.
- Make it easy for your field hosts. Manage and book the travel

logistics and housing arrangements yourself. Make sure the trip complements their long-term work. Find practical ways to bless long-term workers, such as bringing homeschool supplies or special foods they are missing and can't buy there.

- Set aspirational goals and realistic expectations. Review them with your team before the trip, during the trip, and after the trip. Help participants see their own successes in relation to those goals. Help them communicate these goals and successes to supporters.

- Strive to do no harm to the culture or to the long-term work. Bring only the number of people appropriate for the context. Train your team well on culturally appropriate clothing, attitudes, and behaviors to minimize unnecessary attention.

- Debrief often. Intentional debriefing both during the trip and after the trip provides perspective. Short-termers need to glimpse the bigger picture and how their thoughts, feelings, and reactions fit into God's grand plan for themselves, your church, and the world. Ask questions such as the following:
  - "What challenged you most culturally, spiritually, emotionally, or physically?"
  - "How did you experience God there?"
  - "What moment stands out as endearing and significant?"
  - "What difference will your new insight make for society, for your family, for your life, and for the lives of others?"
  - "What is the invitation from God as you move forward from this experience?
  - "What is a one-minute and five-minute inspirational story to share on your return?"

- Plan trips around people and experiences, not primarily around projects. For example, a construction project done by outsiders often makes little financial sense, with foreigners spending thousands of dollars for plane tickets when they could pay local workers instead. These projects utilize unskilled labor when qualified people could be hired, investing in the local economy. Building projects done by Westerners usually don't promote a healthy development model, encouraging the view of Western "knights" riding in on a white horse to save the day for the "village peasants." While making your team members feel good about an accomplishment and promoting team camaraderie, it doesn't usually encourage much interaction with the culture.

After all the work planning a trip with your team, checking the boxes on your list, you'll find yourself on an airplane heading to a foreign country, ready for an adventure with God. Picture yourself as the intentional vision trip leader. You and your team sleep in local homes and drink tea with your host family. You learn your host family's story, pray over them, and experience authentic stories of your own to share later. You interview kingdom-minded field workers who are business leaders, meeting their local employees and purchasing their products. You and your team sit around the dinner table late into the night with a field worker family. Your team experiences firsthand how long-term field workers live, listening to their struggles and joys. As you walk the streets, you and your team observe and pray, meeting people who invite you in for tea. You pray for the sick and pray blessing over their homes. If you have translators, you might even share a story of Jesus.

You climb high monuments and mountains to pray over cities, and shed tears together for the vast un-reachedness of a people group that you now know personally. You participate in conversational English classes and visit schools. You discover leadership traits in yourself you hadn't seen before. And you feel rewarded as you watch your team embrace the primary goals of relationships with locals. You contribute to long-term work when you see your team members' worldviews turned upside down (in a good way!) as they start to consider their long-term role in reaching the nations.

Trip Type #2: Professional Trip

Another type of strategic short-term trip is what I call a *professional trip*. Using a specific skill or profession for a short time to contribute to long-term work can be valuable, and it's an option worth considering, especially if you've already traveled on a vision trip led by an effective team leader.

Ask yourself, *What specialized skills, experience, or education do I have that could kick-start, promote, or enhance a long-term field worker's plans in an unreached area?* Then explore the possibility of taking a team of like-minded professionals—or even going by yourself so you can focus on your contribution. Here are a few ideas for planning a professional trip:

Idea #1: Offer your services at overseas conferences.

Faith-based global organizations hold periodic gatherings to refresh and train their overseas field workers. Are you an IT professional? You can help fix computers for fields workers who have no repair skills. Are you a psychologist? You can lift the spirits of a family in distress. Do you love to bless children? You can serve in a children's program at a conference. I've even heard of a hairstylist who offered free haircuts. She was booked solid!

Idea #2: Offer your specific skill to promote a kingdom business or a long-term field team overseas.

Long-term field workers run businesses, projects, and organizations overseas. Are you an accountant? You can set up a budgeting system for a struggling business. Are you a photographer, writer, or a videographer? You could document an unengaged people group and create resources for prayer or recruiting. Are you a teacher, artist, musician, or sports professional? You could offer a week of training at the invitation of an overseas high school, university, or business organized by the field worker. The point is to connect with a field worker you know, see if your skill would help his or her vision, and go do it.

Idea #3: Join a nonprofit company focused on global work that headquarters in your home country and work for them.

A myriad of roles exist in Western-based nonprofits for you to promote global work behind the scenes, and often require short trips overseas. For example, as a strategist in South Asia for my agency, I organize survey trips for research, visit field workers to assess current realities, and attend overseas conferences to network with key leaders. Field workers also need people like you to visit them and then promote their work to Christians back home.

Idea #4: Volunteer for an international role with your current company.

A Western-based company with international branches may offer opportunities for employees to temporarily relocate overseas to train new employees during the opening of a new branch, for example. While there, you would have a chance to build ongoing relationships with international staff, visit employees' homes, spend a few extra days praying through the city, or meet with field workers in the country to encourage them.

Idea #5: Teach English overseas.

If you live in a Western country, you most likely speak English. As the global language of business, it is a language most of the rest of the world wants to learn. In countries such as India or China, anyone who speaks English can provide a valuable service to the local population by teaching classes in an English-language school while building relationships and experiencing the culture. University students pursuing an internship or a summer experience abroad would do well to search "teaching English abroad" online, along with the name of the country they wish to live in, and then apply.

Idea #6: Study abroad.

If you're a university student pursuing a degree, consider spending a semester abroad. Finish your degree at a university overseas, in England, India, or the United Arab Emirates. I know an intelligent young man applying to become a Fulbright Scholar overseas. Because of his focus on microfinance, he connected to several long-term workers advocating for the urban poor. He hopes to contribute his learning to their long-term work, and they will share with him their passion and experience for the local population and culture. He'll get a year in a country that is less than 2 percent Christian, living out an identity that is completely who God made him to be. By simply rearranging where he gets his degree, he will get cross-cultural experience surrounded by unreached people groups.

Idea #7: Teach a course in a Bible school overseas.

If you're a pastor or spiritual leader, you probably have insight, a particular way of discipling, or experience in leadership training that may be valuable to local believers and leaders in unreached countries. It's helpful to have a trusted contact who personally invites you and knows how your particular teaching will be received. Often, our Western version of leadership, discipleship, even the way we interpret and teach the Bible, doesn't translate effectively because we don't know the language, culture, or worldview of the local country in which we're teaching. So if this is an avenue you're interested in exploring, I'd encourage you to seek out a field worker already on the ground who could advise you.

Cautions for All Professional Trips

As you pray about and consider this second type of short trip, allow me to offer just a few words of caution. Don't go as part of a random vision trip, expecting to use your specific skill. There will be too many agendas at play to make your contribution worthwhile. And don't go without the invitation of a long-term field worker first, or you will not accomplish much and may cause more harm than good.

Also, unless you have decades of experience living overseas, don't go directly to the local population, even if you're partnering with local believers. Even though a local person is a believer or you may be going directly to a local church, lots of misunderstandings and unmet expectations on both sides tend to occur due to a lack of cultural experience and disproportionate income levels. When we have expectations to use our professional skills, we need someone on the ground who knows both cultures well and can be the intermediary to truly make use of those skills during such a short time and also make sure our contribution isn't harmful to the culture. (On vision trips or survey trips, while preferable, it's not necessary to involve a field worker, because those trips are all about learning and relationships, not about *doing*.) So, if done with care and hand in hand with long-term field workers, professionals can provide a much-needed boost to work overseas.

Trip Type #3: Survey Trip

Survey trips, like the trip where we met Cornelius, help us discover strategic and spiritual answers on where to land, how to enter, or who to join long-term. Survey trips uncover possibilities, confirm previous research, and create access into an unknown culture. They lure the explorers of our age, driven to pave a path into a people group unengaged with the gospel. Most vision and professional trips only visit countries that already have enough cross-cultural workers, or to people groups where Jesus is already known. Survey trips do the opposite.

The struggle, of course, in planning a trip to a people and place that is unreached and unengaged is that it is full of unknowns. The unknown screams insecurity, and fear paints pictures of giants in the land. If we are not intentional about where we go on short trips, though, we will end up going to places we already know. We don't tend to go where we don't know, and we certainly don't go where we don't know anyone, which leaves our unengaged people groups—long-term—unengaged.

This is the problem I faced when I first tried to organize that survey trip to the coastal city in India where we found Cornelius. No field workers lived there. No Westerners at that time, in fact. So, no one could pave the way for us or offer us knowledge or help us navigate the culture. The whole trip was full of unknowns. For three years I tried to convince someone to take a survey trip with me, waving around pictures of palm fronds and little Indian boys swimming in the ocean. That's what finally sparked the interest of six brave souls to join me for a two-week trip to a blank-slate city: the unengaged status of the people there, the word "coastal," and a picture of a white beach.

That photo of a white beach led to prayer nights, prayer lunches, and even several days and times of spontaneous group fasting and prayer. We eagerly listened for God's voice. We asked God to speak to us about these ten million people we had read about that didn't have anyone living in their midst, inviting them to follow Jesus.

"They will rebuild the ancient ruins and restore the places long devastated; they will renew the ruined cities that have been devastated for generations," we heard God say to us through the prophet Isaiah (Isa. 58:12). We learned that Islam had first entered India through this city one thousand years ago. The six of us brave, quaking, resolute souls decided that one thousand years was long enough. And so we finally went.

The survey trip ripped the doors of impossibility off of our imaginations. We returned, free from the fear of the unknown, singing the praises of a lovely little city with jungles (yes, it was humid), beaches (yes, lots of people), internet (yes, it was slow)—where people welcomed us and where, yes, a family of Westerners could actually and most certainly live.

Survey Trip Objectives

Most survey trips share the same overall objectives and strategic purposes for the kingdom. Take a look at this list, and, if over half resonate with you, it might be time to plan one!

☐ To make the unknown known
☐ To ask God if you could live there
☐ To gather courage to "break into" a place with no field workers
☐ To gain a "welcome" into that city before someone lands long-term
☐ To research and learn and plan how God might want to engage those people
☐ To envision everyday life in a place with no field workers

- ☐ To encourage more field workers to go where no field workers are
- ☐ To translate the statistics and numbers into actual names and faces
- ☐ To believe that it is possible for people to move there
- ☐ To fall in love with—and advocate for—a people loved by God

Planning Short-Term Trips with Your Church

As leaders and pastors of Western churches get more intentional and strategic about their churches' roles in global work, they often start sending their members on one of these three types of short-term overseas trips we just learned about. They know overseas trips create fresh, hands-on discipleship experiences that propel their members to grow deeper spiritually. People return eager to serve, with a new perspective on God's heart, and a sense of purpose.

Short overseas trips done well—the right type of trip, to a thoughtful location, with good training and effective trip leaders—can also complement a long-term strategic vision for the church to impact unreached people groups across the street and around the world. What if short-term trips organized through our churches inspired people to start working with international students and refugees in our city? What if these trips could discover the long-term field workers sitting in the chairs of our congregations, that the church could raise up, commission, and send to unreached people groups? They can! Let's look at how to plan strategic short-term trips alongside our church leaders.

#1: Remember the first-love syndrome.

People will fall in love with wherever they go first on a trip overseas, so as a church, don't be shy about steering trips toward countries with unreached people groups right from the beginning. Be intentional about highlighting people groups and places with the least access to Jesus. Paul the apostle said, 'My ambition has always been to preach the Good News where the name of Christ has never been heard, rather than where a church has already been started by someone else. I have been following the plan spoken of in the Scriptures, where it says, 'Those who have never been told about him will see, and those who have never heard of him will understand'" (Rom. 15:20–21).

Be cautious about choosing countries close to North American borders for short-term trips. Cheap and close are not the primary criteria on which to measure the intended fruitfulness of a wise trip. Remember to view short-term trips through the lens of your church's long-term global vision. If a nearby country is not where your church hopes to send long-term people, invest long-term, or where most unreached people groups reside, then think twice about going there. Church leaders with high missional intelligence will also not want to invest long-term people or resources in a country already swelling with Western aid and in a country with enough believers already present anyway, so there's no need to send people there short-term.

CHEAP AND CLOSE ARE NOT THE PRIMARY CRITERIA ON WHICH TO MEASURE THE INTENDED FRUITFULNESS OF A WISE TRIP.

Some might argue that because of low expenses and proximity, families can go, and that nearby countries, such as Mexico if a church is in North America, might be a safe first step to attract fearful goers. However, we will probably not expose participants to solid discipleship and community development practices in a country historically saturated with short-term exposure trips, most of which are usually not done well. There are other ways to break down fear of other cultures, right where we live, by interacting with refugees and international students (see chapter 3).

#2: Recruit proactively and individually.

Your church might be the only body of believers dreaming about a city or a people group, or a country or a cause. Pray about people in the church body whom God might draw into his long-term plan to reach the nations. Once God highlights someone to you, personally challenge that person to lead or go on a particular trip. Look especially for believers who are (1) already reaching out to their neighbors and (2) coachable and eager to learn new things. God may highlight specific people when you pray about whom in the church to recruit. That's how the church at Antioch sent their first two long-term field workers:

"One day as these men [the prophets and teachers of the church at Antioch] were worshipping the Lord and fasting, the Holy Spirit said, "Appoint Barnabus and Saul for the special work to which I have called them." So after more fasting and prayer, the men laid their hands on them and sent them on their way." (Acts 13:2–3).

Think about long-term possibilities for the people your church might recruit. Choose your best people, at the quality and level of someone that might be hired on staff at your church. Be open to any age or vocation. Inspire youth, college students, and young adults, but don't forget to call out the fruitful businesspeople, as well as pastors. If pastors with the drive to start a church in their home country catch a vision for planting thousands of churches instead of just one in areas where Christ isn't known, they won't be able to stay where they are. Youth pastors and college pastors would make great field workers too!

#3: Use the trip to mobilize the whole church.

A short-term trip is not just about the trip. By going, we are "putting it on the map" for our church, future supporters, future prayers, and future field workers. Church leaders could plan a sermon series about God's heart for the nations around the timing of a trip. During the Sunday services, video chat with team members overseas in a live feed. Organize all-church global experiences, such as everyone eating refugee rations of rice and beans for a week, while a short-term team visits a refugee camp overseas. Start a private social media feed for the church to follow short-term team members in real time and feel a part of the experience without ever going.

On the team's return, organize a night for friends, supporters, and church members to share stories and photos, including others in their widened worldview and spiritual learning.

#4: Train your people well.

View a short-term trip as a coaching time to disciple people in kingdom ways and Christlikeness. If you do, they will return to the body of believers ready to pour their spiritual growth back into the ones who stayed behind. Right from the start, train participants to view the trip as a six-month experience that includes pre-training, the actual trip, and debriefing time—instead of a two-week experience.

Pre-training allows the church to set expectations, teach useful tools, and shape perspective early, so no one is blindsided when they land. Here are a few types of specialized training to consider, along with the topics you might cover in pre-trip training:

- TEAM DYNAMICS TRAINING: where participants will learn about goals and expectations, the code of conduct, fund-raising, building a prayer team, peacemaking, and personality differences.
- CULTURE TRAINING: which can include topics such as cultural adaptation, worldview, poverty alleviation, community development, social injustice, church-planting models, and identity.
- SPIRITUAL TRAINING: which should focus on God's global heart as

seen through scripture, helping participants understand terms such as *unreached people groups*, and training on how to share Jesus and the good news in honor-shame cultures through telling stories, praying for others, and listening in prayer (make sure to learn about the religious practices of the people group or country you'll visit).

- SAFETY TRAINING: which should include information regarding liability forms, staying out of trouble, getting visas and immunizations, staying healthy, child safety rules, and appropriate gender interactions.

If you're not familiar with content for pre-trip training, you can find most of it in this book. Ask participants to read this book before the trip, and use the questions at the end of each chapter for discussion during team training sessions. For a more detailed training section on each topic, as well as a list of recommended books and movies, visit [[insert URL]].

Often, in trainings, trip leaders use up valuable training time telling about visas, plane tickets, packing, and the logistics of the trip, and answering detailed, boring, and repetitive questions from participants. Instead, put that information in writing so you can use a smaller amount of training time for this. Make the majority of trip training sessions interactive and participatory—exchanging worksheets, lectures, and trip logistics for an experience at the local temple or mosque and a lively discussion.

#5: Encourage Next Steps

A post-trip discussion about what's next often gets postponed or forgotten. But if we train trip members well before we leave, they'll already be looking for ways to maximize the effectiveness of their experience when they return. They'll search for their global role, connect via social media or free phone apps with their new overseas friends, read new books, take classes, or make an international friend locally.

On the trip, perhaps the fortitude and resilience of the field workers touches their heart. Maybe they'll choose to start receiving the field workers' newsletters to encourage and pray for them. Maybe social injustice moves them emotionally. Help them find avenues to volunteer at local nonprofits or learn more about helping address global issues, such as poverty, sex trafficking, or slavery. And if they feel a burden for those who don't know Jesus, encourage them to start making international friends locally, or reaching out to their neighbors.

God willing, a few of the trip takers will sense a spiritual restlessness in their souls, burdened by the faces they met without access to Jesus, waking up in the night and wondering if they were made for *even* more. Could those trip takers surrender their lives full-time to God's calling to the nations? Help them find out! As a church, be glad to unleash them to the nations.

Reflection

1. What experiences do you—or friends you know—have with short-term trips, and how do the descriptions of vision trips, professional trips, or survey trips compare?

2. Write out your journey of experiencing God's heart for the nations, pinpointing defining moments and times of spiritual transformation. What type of trip—as well as where and with whom—would facilitate or advance a long-term global vision for you?

3. If you are leading a trip, or wish to lead a trip, choose a type of trip that matches your goals, brainstorm potential locations and hosts, and develop a recruiting list, training plan, and debriefing plan.

EIGHT

Mobilizing Inspirationally, Giving Extravagantly, and Praying Passionately

I remember the first time I attended a large global conference in Texas, called World Mandate. The intense worship experience left people weeping in the aisles and praying for the glory of God to cover the earth. The Holy Spirit worked through gifted speakers to pierce hearts with conviction. Hundreds of young people streamed down the aisles to surrender their lives to go to the nations. After hearing of a specific financial need, the offering plates filled to overflowing, and thousands joyfully gave to long-term church planters living overseas. The prayer room filled with students pouring out their hearts to God on behalf of people groups in places with no gospel witness. They read scripture, drew prophetic pictures, and gathered in small circles, praying over maps and photos, unaware that hours had passed.

The worship leaders, speakers, executives, and administrative people who organize and promote events like this inspire and mobilize people to go to the nations. The generous givers provide financially for those who go to the nations. And the people praying on their knees stir up the heavenlies to action on behalf of the people who go.

These mobilizers, givers, and prayers form an essential army of *stayers*. They serve vital roles in reaching the nations for the glory of God by creating bridges between "here" and "there." To win souls from every language, tribe, and nation, *every* follower of Jesus must discover his or her God-ordained role and get involved. Similarly, it takes more kinds of people to win a war or even a national football game than just the soldiers or the players. It takes generals and coaches, strategists and scorekeepers, and people cheering at home and on the sidelines, contributing the best of themselves toward a common purpose.

Perhaps you were made to pursue God's heart for the nations with a specific supporting role. You may be made to mobilize. You may be made to give. You may be made to pray. Whichever you are called to do, do it well, and do it with all your heart, mind, and strength.

Become an Inspirational Mobilizer

What is a mobilizer? Those who desire to see other people inspired, recruited, trained, and released into an important calling. In Numbers 10:1–2, we see a model of what mobilizers do when the Lord said to Moses, "Make two silver trumpets of hammered silver for calling the community to assemble and for signaling the breaking of camp." One trumpet called everyone to pay attention, and the other sounded to direct the troops. This is the essence of a mobilizer's work: helping average Christians notice the rest of the world and discover their roles in an extraordinary cause, and then creating small steps for them to move into those roles. This might look like offering small-group global experiences by leading short-term trips, cross-cultural internships, and nations-focused small groups. Or, it might be organizing the Worldwide Perspectives course, or a variation of it, at our church—or inviting inspirational field workers to speak at our church services.

Or it could be creating all-church nations prayer nights and weeklong global challenges in which church members can participate right at home. The possibilities are numerous, and mobilization efforts can look different from person to person.

Take Drew, for example. Drew is a model mobilizer. He's a champion of causes and calls the church body's attention to the nations with a proverbial trumpet in one hand by keeping focus on the nations. In his other hand, he holds a virtual trumpet that directs the movement of individual believers toward the nations by creating ways to get involved.

When Drew speaks, people want to be part of whatever he's promoting, coordinating, or organizing. By believing in their potential, he makes people come alive. He exudes positivity and possibility. He creates practice paths for the disciples who answer his rallying call. This practicing gives his disciples a chance to try, to fail, and to learn from it. He encourages them to get up again, believing they can reach whatever finish line the Holy Spirit inspires them to run toward.

"As long as I can catalyze more goers to the field than just myself," said Drew, "then with God's help, I'll keep staying. Once God removes that favor from me, my family will go."

Drew works on the global outreach team at a large church where he and his wife lead a network of cross-cultural internships. They mobilize by modeling the making of disciples who make disciples, reaching out to internationals right around them. Of the dozens of people they've mentored, more than half of them now live overseas as full-time field workers in unreached people groups, and the rest are reaching out right where they live.

"Someone must sound the rallying call," said Phil Parshall, field worker and author. "Mobilizers stir other Christians to active concern for reaching the world. They coordinate efforts between senders, the local churches, sending agencies, and workers on the field. Mobilizers are essential!"[1]

Frontiers founder and gifted mobilizer Greg Livingstone recruited a few brave souls to go to the ends of the earth through his fledgling organization more than thirty years ago. Now Frontiers sends thousands of field workers from almost fifty countries to more than fifty Muslim countries—inviting Muslims, with love and respect, to follow Jesus.

As a mobilizer Livingstone still says the same things to those considering a life overseas. In a speech to a group of Frontiers Mobilizers, he affirmed the uniqueness of apostolic people destined to forge new spiritual paths in the direst places, saying, "You're a swan in a lake full of ducks. What's your unique role in the greatest rescue operation of all time? Get a dream and get a team!" He challenges anyone who will listen to reach for a higher purpose in life, saying, "Give up your small ambitions. What do *you* believe God for? What does *God* have planned for the rest of your life? The reward is great and the cost is high. Come and die!"

Livingstone also inspires other mobilizers by counseling them, "Find out where the fish are biting and fish there. 'Come' works better than 'go.' Keep a list of the top ten unreached peoples and places you believe God for. Pray about those ten, and talk about them to everyone you meet."

Sometimes those in mobilization roles are more introverted and systematic, serving in the background more than being out in front of people, like those with more charismatic, outgoing personalities. I'm thinking of Bill.

Bill uses his executive administrative skills to lead in a field preparation department at a large sending agency. His never-give-up, just-keep-swimming persistence—as well as his ability to develop structures—created a trustworthy path for entire teams of field workers to partner with churches to go together to the nations. In fact, in the last twenty-five years, he and the field preparation department coached and helped send seventy-one teams to more than thirty countries with unreached people groups—thirty-two of those teams packaged as entire teams from specific churches.

Are you a mobilizer? You might be! Maybe you naturally mobilize people and champion causes. Perhaps you've already found the section "How to Use *Across the Street and Around the World*" in the back of this book, with the outline for a four-week sermon series, and you've also discovered the twelve-week small group plan. Maybe you're already thinking of ordering extra copies of this book to give to decision makers in your church.

Does it sound like I'm shamelessly promoting this book? I am! God made me a natural mobilizer too. I can't help it. I wrote this book to mobilize the Western church to get involved in a thoughtful, purposeful, and fruitful way to see all unreached people groups know Jesus Christ.

Everyone can mobilize others to care about people in other cultures, but God also gifts some people to mobilize full-time—on staff at a church or at the headquarters of a global missions organization. As we consider these possibilities together, let's spend some time praying about practicing inspirational mobilization:

God, help me to inspire other Christians toward this great cause of reaching those farthest from you with the good news of Jesus Christ. Give me passion. Expand my influence. Salt my speech. Help me to develop structures that can spark and sustain a global interest, for adults, youth, and children. Show me practically how to involve my family, my small group, and my church, inspiring them to wake up to God's global heart.

Become an Extravagant Giver

Another important *staying* role is that of an extravagant giver. "You can't take it with you," wrote author and pastor Randy Alcorn in *The Treasure Principle*, a book about the reality of heavenly rewards and the wisdom of investing in heavenly treasure. "But you *can* send it on ahead."[2]

Jesus agreed: "Don't store up treasures here on earth, where moths eat them and rust destroys them, and where thieves break in and steal. Store your treasures in heaven, where moths and rust cannot destroy, and thieves do not break in and steal. Wherever your treasure is, there the desires of your heart will also be" (Matt. 6:19–21).

We are all simply stewards and managers of God's money. "By clinging to what isn't ours," Alcorn said, "we forgo the opportunity to be granted ownership in heaven. By generously distributing God's property here on earth, we will become property owners in heaven!"[3]

A successful businessman stood in front of a small group of men and women committed to moving overseas. He declared with much enthusiasm, "I'm Jay. And I exist to fund the Great Commission!" I had never heard *that* before. Jay said he embraced this role fifteen years earlier when God blessed the work of his hands in businesses that he had started.

"I love to give!" he announced joyfully. "I work hard to be profitable in business so I can give more. I don't say this to brag. I just don't think people talk about it enough." He told of a weekend when he went away to wrestle with God about a vision statement for his life. He returned with a scrap of paper and these compelling words: "Jay exists to fund the Great Commission." He signed it and aligned all his efforts and energy with this goal.

Jay explained that he gave generously even when he didn't have money. "I noticed the more I gave away, the more money my business made. Maybe God saw I would be faithful to give generously, when I only had a little. He could see my heart was all in on this vision statement for my life. He saw he could entrust me with more, and I would keep giving more. Then I just kept making more money, so that I could give more."

When his business sold for $5 million, he invested much of it in Alcorn's and Jesus' treasure principle by funding the Great Commission (Matt. 28:19–20). His heavenly investment is right now compounding interest.

When we are called as givers who sow into the expansion of God's kingdom, we need to do it generously, intentionally, and wisely, as Jay does. Like him, we can make sure to research organizations, request updates on the work, and visit workers on the field. We can also purposely give where church-planting efforts are vastly under-resourced, directing our funding to organizations and field workers introducing the gospel to people groups with the least access to Jesus. And in all of our giving, we should proceed with as much wisdom as possible.

Donated money is like fire in other people's hands. It can light a candle on a dark night. Or it can burn down a building. If I may, I'd like to offer a word of caution. Sometimes, in our inexperience and zeal, we think that if a local, overseas organization just had more money, it would solve everything, and if we cut out the "middleman" from our home country, like America, we would save a bunch of money. Not necessarily. Giving can cause harm when we as Westerners directly fund a local organization or local church in a country far away from ours. Most of the time we don't know the culture, the language, or the situation well enough to introduce money in an informed way. Many a generous donor giving to evangelistic efforts falls into the trap of wanting more bang for their buck, so they give through local organizations or churches across the sea for "only fifty dollars a month." But money from uninformed foreigners can stir up jealousy between local Christian organizations, promote dependency on outsiders, and stifle indigenous initiatives.

So what do you do if you have money to give and you want to give it to affect people halfway around the world? Introducing funding works best when there is accountability and transparency from someone on the ground who knows *both* cultures well—someone from your own culture who lives and works long-term in that country and knows how the funding can best be distributed honorably, ethically, and effectively. Without that link, reporting on the use of funding also becomes challenging. When giving to a ministry, it's important to know the structures in place for accurate reporting of financials and results, and it's best done through someone in your own culture, who works in the culture you're trying to affect. So, as givers, let's be "as shrewd as snakes and harmless as doves" (Matt. 10:16), making sure we combine our spiritual fervor with wise business practices and good cultural sensitivity. Yes, give generously, but also give intelligently.

DONATED MONEY IS LIKE FIRE IN OTHER PEOPLE'S HANDS. IT CAN LIGHT A CANDLE ON A DARK NIGHT. OR IT CAN BURN DOWN A BUILDING.

OBSERVATIONS BY THE TRAVELING TEAM

- Evangelical Christians could provide all of the funds needed to plant a church in each of the 6,900 unreached people groups with only 0.03 percent of their income.
- The Church has roughly 3,000 times the financial resources

and 9,000 times the manpower needed to finish the Great Commission.[4]

- If every evangelical gave 10 percent of their income to missions we could easily support 2 million new field workers.

Let's pause and take an inventory of our giving habits. Are we giving in a way that earns a return on investment in heaven? Make a list of how much you give and where it goes each month. How does your giving compare to the average giving for Christians in chapter 6? What is your attitude toward your income and toward giving?

After we assess our giving practices, we may find ourselves worried about providing for ourselves or for our families and unable to even dream about giving generously. Perhaps we're living paycheck to paycheck, just making enough to pay our bills and slowly reduce our debts. It's wise to focus on getting financially healthy. In this season, we can ask God to give us assurance that he cares enough for us to provide for our needs as we focus on kingdom living, and just start giving a little bit in faith to start.

Jesus said, "Don't worry about these things, saying, 'What will we eat? What will we drink? What will we wear?' These things dominate the thoughts of unbelievers, but your heavenly Father already knows all your needs. Seek the Kingdom of God above all else, and live righteously, and he will give you everything you need" (Matt. 6:31–33).

On the other hand, if we find ourselves feeling tight-fisted about investing our resources in growing the kingdom, even though we may have the funds, then we can ask God to loosen our grip on what he has given us.

Let's pray this prayer together to grow into generous givers:

Lord, you know my attitude toward money. You know my fears about my current and future provision. You know the reasons I give the amount that I do. You also know the amount of treasure

*already stored up for me in heaven. I want to acknowledge that
everything I have is yours and is a gift from you. Thank you.
Please show me how you would like me to steward and manage
the resources you've given me and what part you want me to play
in giving to see the nations reached.*

Become a Passionate Prayer Raiser

What is a prayer raiser? Put simply, prayer raisers pray for the nations.
And they raise up other people to pray. They know the Lord listens to
the cries and prayers of God's people. God's heart is already eager for
a remnant from every nation to come back into relationship with him.
So prayer raisers plead with God on behalf of people like the millions of
Arabs in Sudan, asking for the peace that comes through Jesus Christ.
They cry with God over the displaced and persecuted minority group
Rohingya in Myanmar and Bangladesh, asking him to intervene with
the justice of heaven as they flee killing, rape, and torture. When we
pray like this, and gather others to pray, our hearts start to beat in sync
with God's heart for the world, and he is often pleased to act.

To raise up prayer, we must first believe that God allows us to
participate in how life on earth unfolds, even when we're far away
from people and world events. Moses, Abraham, Hezekiah, Jonah, and
others in the Bible actually changed God's mind on different matters
(Gen. 18:23–33; Ex. 32:14; Jer. 26:19; Jon. 3:10). Daniel, Elijah, and
the apostles actively prayed for heavenly intervention in earthly situations (1 Kings 18:20–40; Dan. 10:12; Acts 19:12).

To build this kind of faith, we start by praying for situations
and people right around us. The more we notice prayer impacting
our own lives, the more faith we will have to pray for God's will in
places with little Christian influence. We'll grow confidence to also

ask God on behalf of field workers in challenging places for things such as difficult-to-get visas, intervention during unexplained spiritual attacks, and perseverance during persecution.

The apostle James reminded us that "the earnest prayer of a righteous person has great power and produces wonderful results" (James 5:16). If this is true, prayer is powerful. When it doesn't appear powerful—that is, when the results don't match up—then we need to approach it as we would any other discipline. Ask questions, learn from others, and keep praying until we begin experiencing the truth about prayer found in the Bible.

Fruitfulness, Discipline, and Power in Prayer

Daniel Waheli, who wrote *Lessons Learned in the Lion's Den: Imprisoned for Sharing Jesus*, said much of his fruitfulness, which included a role in many thousands coming to faith in Jesus in several movements in Africa, comes from praying.[5] He spends as much time reading God's Word, worshiping, and enjoying Jesus in prayer now that he has moved back to his home country as he did when he lived overseas.

Daniel spends about 10 percent of his waking time with Jesus, he says humbly, a constant smile creasing the corners of his eyes. When asked how this is possible since he has much leadership responsibility, he smiles again and says he wakes early and spends about an hour reading and studying God's Word. After breakfast, he listens to worship music, talking and listening to Jesus as he exercises for another hour or so. This seems like something you and I could actually do too, praying for fruitfulness in work overseas.

Hudson Taylor affirmed the absolute necessity of prayer as foundational for fruitfulness in China. He wrote, "Brother, if you would enter that Province, you must go forward on your knees."[6] In fact, all church-planting movements include a backdrop of abundant, excessive prayer. "The one absolute prerequisite for progress in this endeavor [church-planting movements] is praying until the impossible happens," wrote Jerry Trousdale in *Miraculous Movements: How Hundreds of Thousands of Muslims are Falling in Love With Jesus.*[7] We can partner with the Hudson Taylors of our day by praying for their work, even half a world away.

Praying for fruitfulness in unreached people groups requires us to believe the name of Jesus has power. Jesus said, "But if you remain in me and my words remain in you, you may ask for anything you want, and it will be granted! (John 15:7). This is not an automatic wish-granting situation. It has to do with abiding in Jesus so much that our wills are intertwined with his. We know him. We can hear him.

Richard Foster, in *Celebration of Discipline,* agreed when he wrote, "To ask 'rightly' involves transformed passions. In prayer, real prayer, we begin to think God's thoughts after him; to desire the things he desires, to love the things he loves, to will the things he wills. Progressively, we are taught to see things from his point of view."[8]

Daniel Waheli's confidence in Christ is expressed in his simple, powerful declaration of God's truths. With an unwavering belief that prayer invites God's will on earth, he bolsters other Christians who have only ever settled on untested, shallow prayers. Those who pray with Daniel start to pray more boldly along the lines of the will of God. And it is God's will that his kingdom will come on earth as it is in heaven, in every nation and corner of the world.

The discipline of prayer raising that Daniel Waheli practices with others requires perseverance—an elusive trait in our instant-gratification world. We need to view prayer as essential and important global work, right here at home, and approach it with dogged persistence. Paul the apostle wrote, "Pray in the Spirit at all times and on every occasion. Stay alert and be persistent in your prayers for all believers everywhere" (Eph. 6:18).

Why must we stay alert and persistent in our prayer life for believers everywhere, especially those entering places where the gospel is not known? Because our common enemy, Satan, and his minions will not give up long-held territories in spiritually dark places of the world without a fight in the heavenlies. "For we are not fighting against flesh-and-blood enemies, but against evil rulers and authorities of the unseen world, against mighty powers in this dark world, and against evil spirits in the heavenly places" (Eph. 6:12).

Recently, during a forty-day fast, Daniel Waheli felt compelled by God and confirmed by godly leaders to start a continuous, worldwide prayer movement. He believes God is asking us to fast and pray round-the-clock for the next ten years for 10 percent of the Muslim world to come to Jesus. More than one thousand years ago, a group of monks called the Moravians prayed nonstop for a hundred years, birthing a breakthrough of the gospel into many previously unfruitful lands. Why not again? Since the beginning of 2018, a grassroots initiative has sprung up all around the world, in various organizations and churches. Anyone can sign in to this growing movement to participate even one day a month at www.1010prayerandfasting.com.

Creativity, Structure, and Consistency in Prayer

I remember when I caught the vision for prayer and wanted to pray more and invite others to pray for the nations. At first, I didn't understand how people could get together and pray for a whole hour at a time, or even a whole night, without getting bored. I've since experienced that prayer for the nations can be fun, interactive, and creative, done in a way where we're not stuck listening to one person recite a monologue to God while everyone else falls asleep.

Every month, a group of our friends who love to pray for India gets together at someone's house for several hours. We bring things like crayons, flip charts, maps, guitars, and bongo drums. Sometimes we spread the maps out on the floor and place our hands on specific cities, asking God how he sees those cities and what he wants to do there. Another time we might color pictures that God shows us about specific field workers, places, or situations in India when we quiet ourselves to listen. Then we share our pictures with one another and agree in prayer, sometimes discovering encouraging things to share with field workers in that region later.

Another idea for group prayer for the nations is to write verses that come to mind or scrawl lies of the enemy in black marker on scraps of paper and then use the verses to speak truth over lies. We might tear up the papers with the lies on them as we declare God's truth. One time, we even dragged out a box of Legos to corporately build as we prayed over a city where few workers lived—a bridge to symbolize a new way into the city and a wall, with angels on top, to protect the few workers living there now, for example.

We often worship during our group prayer times, stopping after each phrase of a song, to use the words over specific situations or field workers we know living in India. Short video clips on the news or from www. prayercast.com help inform our prayers about India's Hindus, Muslims, Buddhists, Sihks, and Jains. We, and our children, wave flags while we sing the promises of God over injustice, such as child slavery, poverty, or caste prejudice, in colors that represent qualities of the kingdom. White for purity. Purple for royalty and our position as sons and daughters of the King. Red for love. We include our children because we are prayer raisers, motivated to raise up children who know how to pray fervently, effectively, and with power for God's kingdom to come to all peoples.

Some people who pray for the nations and invite others to do so are more systematic and structured in their prayer life. My mom and dad, for example, prefer to sit together after breakfast and enjoy a passage of scripture before they close their eyes and talk to God, or take a walk and talk to God. They tell him what is on their hearts for specific people and places.

My parents keep a notebook full of field workers' Christmas cards, as well as a Rolodex with prayer cards for all the field workers they know and the disciples they've trained over the years. Each day they pray for a different field worker and a different person or family. They pray for each of their children and grandchildren almost every morning, too, asking God for protection, spiritual understanding, and a close relationship with Jesus for each of us.

In the back of their one-hundred-year-old red barn, there's a room that used to hold hay for horses. My dad transformed it into a map room. Books line the dusty shelves next to a single rocking chair beneath a hanging light bulb, the kind you turn on with a pull string. His many scribbled-in journals and his precious Bible, with every space covered in ink on its brittle pages, stand side by side with numerous missionary biographies.

Maps, globes, and pins on strategic locations serve as reminders of peoples and places that still need gospel messengers. As my parents look at their maps and globes and pray through the people groups featured in *Operation World*, a comprehensive book of all the unreached peoples of the world, they ask God to stir more long-term field workers to go to the least reached.[9]

Whether we are more creative or systematic in prayer, finding a consistent time to pray means that we'll actually do it, developing a habit of prayer. As we pray consistently and regularly about people on the other side of the world, we feel closer to them. We know more about them—so we care more—and then we pray even more—and raise up others to pray even more.

Are You a Passionate Prayer Raiser?

If you're thinking about how little time you devote to prayer for the world or about your inexperience with prayer, be encouraged. No one climbs Mount Everest the first day. No one learns to play the piano with one lesson. Intercessory prayer is the same. It takes practice. Find a daily structure to consistently pray through a people group list just a few minutes each day and give it a try.

Let's ask God to grow in us a desire for passionate prayer, and for raising up others to pray for the nations:

God, please give me a heart for prayer. Help me want to pray. Give me discipline to set aside quiet, secret time to spend with you. Let me hear the Shepherd's voice, so I can pray with your heart and know your will. Foster creativity in me to interact with you about the nations in exciting ways that aren't boring. Open my spiritual eyes to see where you are and to observe what you are doing in the world and how you are answering.

People who practice God's heart for the nations usually do all three of these staying roles—mobilizing, giving, and praying—in varying degrees. As we experiment, we might find ourselves coming alive inside, burning with energy and passion, every time we do something related to one of these three areas. If so, throw yourself into it wholeheartedly because this just might be what you were made to do as a light to the whole world.

Reflection

1. How has your soul come to life when you tried some of these important staying roles: mobilizing, giving and praying? What seemed to work well?
2. What is God saying to you about how you can mobilize, give, or pray for the nations? Scan through each section, and find one idea from each of the three areas to try.

PART THREE

Around the World

*Discovering If You
Could Go to the
Ends of the Earth*

NINE

Wrestling with Calling, Gifting, and Personalities

I sat cross-legged on the floor of a Bedouin-style tent, eating couscous and camel with my hands from a common platter alongside North African Arabs. With the Saharan heat drifting in, my short-term team and I laughed with our Bedouin hosts and talked of this Jesus we followed, who taught that when someone sues you for your shirt, you should say, "Here. Take my coat too." Later, when one of the men on our team failed to find a suitable African burnoose, a traditional hooded cloak, to take home, one of our new Bedouin friends said, "Here. I have two. You can have one of them." He grinned and winked, "That's the kind of thing you told me your Jesus would do."

In stifling heat and desert sand only a few hours from an al-Qaeda training camp, I was wrapped three times in a *mulafa*, a long cotton sheet worn by the Muslim women in that area. And I felt freer than I had ever felt in America. *Could I possibly live in some strategic place overseas like this, God?* I prayed. *What do I have to do to make that happen?* I figured I would just buy a plane ticket and go! *But would I be able to actually live overseas longer than a few weeks?* I frowned.

Back home in America, just a week after returning from that cross-cultural vision trip, I gazed out at our perfectly manicured lawn, watching our youngest child play. A cloudless blue sky and dreamy sun shone down on our four-bedroom home in a master-planned community. Our Phoenix suburb was touted as one of the safest places in America. The smell of summer grilling wafted through the neighborhood, and I could hear the compelling jingle of the ice-cream truck making its afternoon rounds. The Sahara seemed faraway and completely unreal.

I pictured my husband, hunched in a swivel chair and crammed into a cubicle at that very moment, fingers poised on the keyboard, staring at a thousand unread emails. I felt the four walls of his cloth-covered cubicle plastic closing in on my soul like a coffin. *What are we doing here, Lord? Working to live and living to work, just to have a nice, comfortable life? Surely you have more in mind for our lives as followers of you?*

Then I remembered sitting one Sunday in the comfortable, theater-style seats of our church during service, watching yet another clip of a natural disaster killing thousands overseas, accompanied by pleas for prayers and funds. It had happened in Pakistan, a country where few Christ followers live and where Westerners can't easily enter. Muslims in countries like Pakistan live their whole lives without ever experiencing a God who could draw near to them and offer them life here and forever.

The pastor had preached about Peter, the disciple who asked Jesus if he could walk on water and then did it. Jesus had told Peter to follow him, and Peter dropped his fishing nets and did it. How could I sit there in that comfortable place and *do nothing*?

I quelled the welling up in my heart as I sat on my back patio. Could an ordinary couple with children living in suburban America really do anything of significance globally long-term?

My cell phone rang. "You're late picking me up from my friend's house!" my daughter said, her voice clearing the global angst from my thoughts.

The immediacy of everyday life crowded my global daydreaming to a faraway space. The welling up of holy dissatisfaction floundered as my vision filled with bills, a house payment, the busy activities of four children, and a husband who just laughed when I suggested insane things, like moving overseas. My perception of reality created a rather impassable chasm between my suburbs and my Sahara.

I never could have imagined that, four years later, my husband and I would quit our jobs and sell our house and everything we owned. Soon after, we would find ourselves living in a bright-green house on the edge of the jungles of India, on the outskirts of a city of a million people. Our family would land in the middle of a sea of nine million Muslims—the population of the entire state of New Jersey—who had never been introduced to Jesus Christ as the way to God.

The Apostolic Yearning

You might experience this same restlessness within your own heart too as you open yourself up to the world beyond your doorstep. Often, an experience, a message, a book, the world news, or an interaction with a person from another country fosters a willingness to consider radical participation with the world in a way you might never before have considered.

This angst often includes a recurring global wondering in the back of your mind, perhaps even unearthing a buried desire to be involved across cultures in a meaningful, spiritual way. These thoughts prick the soul of what we'll call an apostolic person. God shapes an apostolic person to pave new, untrod paths to cross cultures with the good news of the kingdom of God. The last chapters of this book will help us discover if we are the kind of genuine, humble Jesus followers that God might choose to send overseas someday. It's about revisiting the way we think and act to find out if our souls, minds, and actions align with the character—and willingness—of someone who can thrive living in other cultures.

Hopefully, soon we'll be able to realistically ask, with the confidence that comes from practical experience and the transformation of mind and soul, "God, would you consider sending me?"

Whenever someone begins to ask this question, some rocks along the path to a life overseas need to be removed. These obstacles might have stopped *you* from even asking this question. They usually begin with "But what about . . ." or "But I'm not . . ." These misconceptions about people who live and work cross-culturally are exactly that: misconceptions. So let's look at the common objections together and learn the truth behind the misconception.

Objection #1: The Question of Gifting

Perhaps you think people who move overseas in the name of Jesus are so much more naturally gifted than you are, that they are superstars. They pray all day, regularly lead people to God in a winsome way, live in huts in the heat, eat fish heads without complaining, and speak three languages fluently. Yes and no. Many cross-cultural workers *do* fit this description . . . after years! None of them started out this way—none at all.

Most cross-cultural workers are just ordinary people who, time after time, decide to take one more step in a certain direction to see what would happen. Maybe it started in seventh grade when they heard a field worker speak about tribal animists in Papua New Guinea. Something stirred inside of them. Maybe a teenager came alive when she took a trip to another country with her youth group. A college student who studied abroad and felt the yearning for a life of purpose in other cultures. A young adult who took college classes that inspired him to choose a job in Malawi over a summer sweetheart in Malibu. An adult who read global books, took global classes, or supported a field worker as a spark of interest in the nations grew.

These people didn't just wake up one day and board a plane the next because they felt supernaturally gifted to do so. They each took a hundred small steps in an intentional direction—small steps that formed their characters, their perseverance, their skills, and their abilities to hear the Shepherd's voice guiding them. They trained themselves to become the sort of people God could send overseas as his ambassadors of the kingdom of Heaven to other nations. And this is something we can do as well.

God fans the apostolic question—the yearning inside—when we choose to step into the waters of the Jericho, not knowing if the waters will part. We can be just like the leader Joshua, who obeyed when God told him that the waters of the river his people needed to cross would part only when they took the first step (Josh. 3:13). They took a step. And one more. And then another. Perhaps the question of gifting is more a question of perseverance.

But while the idea of being gifted enough or already fully equipped and ready to live overseas is built on a faulty premise, it is still wise to discover our more specific spiritual gifting, because we use our spiritual gifting anywhere we're planted.

If you're a teacher, teach. In Tennessee or Timbuktu, teach. If your spiritual gifting is encouragement, encourage. In Louisiana or Laos, encourage others. If your spiritual gifting is serving, serve. In Maine or Manu, serve others. Spiritual gifting is what we do anywhere God plants, or replants, us.

When I mention gifting, one question

SPIRITUAL GIFTING IS WHAT WE DO ANYWHERE GOD PLANTS, OR REPLANTS, US.

that comes up often is the worry that we may lack a gift for learning languages, which can be a legitimate concern. But what I've found is that anyone can learn another language—if we put the time in, immerse ourselves in the culture, and persevere. Getting a poor grade in high school Spanish isn't an indicator of our inability to learn a language. In fact, most field workers didn't think they could learn another language either. But they did.

With modern language learning methods and interactive language schools located in host countries, we can learn conversation before reading and writing.[1] We listen first and then gradually experiment with basic words that we string together, growing into participating members of the community. In just a few weeks of full-time language learning, we'll head to the market and say, "Bread. Want. Hungry. Price?" Pretty soon after that, we might be able to say, "I buy bread now, please." In another six months, we'll be sharing stories with our language teachers about how we make bread with our mothers—and then praying for *their* mothers. After a year or two, we'll be sipping tea while discussing Jesus Christ, the Bread of Life.

One day, we might find ourselves sharing Jesus with a rickshaw driver, a stick of chicken liver in our hands, sweat forming rivulets down our backs, surprised that we're actually here. If we live with our hearts open to taking small steps and saying yes, we might cross a bridge stretching all the way from our suburbs to the Sahara God has designed for us to influence.

Objection #2: The Question of Calling

"But I don't know if I'm *called* to move overseas," is a common objection I hear about crossing cultures. After all, God called the apostle Paul with a light from heaven on his way to Damascus, striking him blind in his path. Jesus himself audibly spoke to Paul with specific instructions. Later, he further revealed a special purpose for him: "But the Lord said, 'Go, for Saul is my chosen instrument to take my message to the Gentiles and to kings, as well as to the people of Israel'" (Acts 9:15).

Are you waiting for something as significant as a lightning bolt before you allow yourself to consider moving overseas?

Most cross-cultural workers do not experience such a clear directive. Many of them *do* have clear and memorable moments of submission to God's will in their lives. They also know that God revealed to them, in various ways and times, their unique and specific purpose. But all of those confirmations and experiences with God are painted in different shades.

Most future field workers receive these confirmations along the way, as they actively move along the path toward a life in another culture. If you're waiting for a call, a sign, or a miracle that will unequivocally compel you down a global path before you risk stepping out in faith, you may be waiting a long time.

Instead of waiting for a green light before you move forward, why not take forward-moving steps until a red light compels you to stop? Instead of requiring a clear direction to *go*, could it be instead you need clear direction to *stay*? Jesus already makes it quite clear what he thinks about this.

When I read Matthew 28, I imagine Jesus gathering his eager and wondering disciples just before he disappeared into the clouds back to heaven. In today's vernacular it might sound something like this:

"Let's be very clear about what I'd like you to do. No parables this time. Go! Go into the whole world! You've experienced and seen good news these past three years, so pass that on to everyone. You know how I've taught you, so go figure out how to teach everyone else to obey all of it. By the way, make sure that the people you are teaching to obey me (and thus obey God) are covered with knowledge of God the Father, and of me, and of the Spirit that I'm sending you for power. Baptize them to symbolize their surrender."

Then the disciples nodded and said, "Of course. Thanks for the clear instructions."

"But where should we go? To whom should we go?" one might have asked Jesus.

Jesus answered, while the clouds started to part, "To the suburbs of your hometown of Jerusalem, of course. But also Samaria, your next-door neighbors whom you despise and certainly don't know very well. And just in case you feel like you only have Jerusalem and Samaria, then let me spell it out: you've got to get to the ends of the earth, to everyone, to all the people groups, to all the nations!"

I can imagine them, this meager number of eleven disciples, their faces clouded with the impossibility of such a task. Jesus says knowingly, "Yes, this is too hard and too impossible, but go, because I'll be with you, even to the very end of the age!" (adaptation of Matt. 28:18–20).

Consider acting on Jesus' suggestion—oh, I mean his command— for you to go make disciples of all the nations of the world. With the desperate lack of believers willing to go despite the clear command to go, if you're willing, start down the path!

The first question you might ask is, "If I'm supposed to go, *where* are you calling me to go, God?" Since *go* is a verb, it's logical to seek God for a calling to a specific place, usually informed by your past experience. You might pray, "I had a Spanish tutor from Peru, God. I really liked him. Should I go to Peru? I know a teacher in the Philippines. I'm a teacher. Is it the Philippines, God? India seems the most unreached; should I go there, God?"

Yes, eventually, you must ask God to give you direction on where. (By the way, the *where* will change over time.) But calling is probably not a *where*. It's probably a *who*. So, instead, first ask *who*. "God, if you are anointing me to cross cultures, to *whom* are you calling me to be an apostle of good news?"

The disciples-turned-apostles Peter and Paul knew *who*. Paul wrote, "For the same God who worked through Peter as the apostle to the Jews also worked through me as the apostle to the Gentiles" (Gal. 2:8). Paul said it again in Romans: "God has appointed me as the apostle to the Gentiles" (Rom. 11:13). Paul then traveled all over the civilized world where Gentiles lived, led by both the Spirit and strategy.

The next (or if you're a millennial, maybe the first) question you might ask is, "With whom can I go?" You are called to go to the ends of the earth *with others*! You don't have to do it alone. A collection of people with your same passion, drive, and desire to go are just waiting to discover you. While precious few field workers might be living among an unreached people group, when the few who are there see you coming, they'll shower you with welcome, ready to coach and encourage you in the field.

Once you narrow the *who* down to people groups within an unreached block, like Muslims, Hindus, Buddhists, animists, or the unreligious, contact a mission agency that sends to those peoples (see chapter 5). They'll connect you to others on your same journey. You'll encourage one another, band together, and go together to the field. More people would also consider moving overseas if someone they know personally invited them—you! Could you envision this journey with a specific friend or two by your side? Ask them to take a small step of yes with you.

Try praying through the *who* . . . and the *with whom*.

Lord, help me to shed my view that I must be "called" in a supernatural way. Expand my vision, God, of what you could do through me in the world. Help me pursue the who by filling my dreams and prayers with information about peoples with the least access to you. Give me like-minded friends to join me on this journey. Thank you that I don't have to go alone, because you mean for me to join others, coached by someone one step ahead of me. Guide me one small step at a time.

Objection #3: The Question of Personality

"I'm no Mother Teresa," some might say. "I don't even like to be around sick people, and I don't care that much about poor people. I'm not really a camping-type person either. I don't see myself living in a hut in the jungle."

When it comes to overseas missions, we hear about Christians who work with people living in poverty, maybe living in the slums, a village, or with a tribe in the mountains. This tends to lead people into thinking that we have to be a certain kind of person to participate in God's work in the world. What may surprise us is that cross-cultural workers wear all shades of personalities, and their way of working in other cultures varies with their God-given personalities. There must be room in overseas ministry for more than just the Bleeding Hearts. I want to inspire the Strategic Thinkers, the Obedient Disciples, the Adventure Travelers, and the Meaning and Purpose people, too.

The Bleeding Heart

"I just want to help someone!" a Bleeding Heart pleads.

For years, I never really understood this type of person, and I sometimes questioned their authenticity. Are they really *that* unselfish? I'm a fairly selfish person. I find it hard to imagine someone *wanting* to wash dishes, *wanting* to bandage someone's oozing sores, or *wanting* to help someone move furniture. I'll do these things, but I don't really want to.

But these Bleeding Hearts love to help. It's what makes them feel most fulfilled. When they help someone, they're actually living in their sweet spot—in their zone—the way God designed them to be. Bleeding Hearts often consider overseas work, because they know that people living in poverty need help. Countries slammed with natural disasters need help. Orphans need help. Widows need help.

Mother Teresa, who brought the dying of Calcutta off the streets and washed their bodies, said, "Being unwanted, unloved, uncared for, forgotten by everybody, I think that is a much greater hunger, a much greater poverty than the person who has nothing to eat."[2]

I'd like to say to Bleeding Hearts, you don't need to become a nurse to make a difference overseas. In fact, becoming a nurse so that you can move overseas to save the world will most likely lead to burnout as you try to drain the ocean with a teacup.

Instead, Bleeding Hearts can team up with Strategic Thinkers and study community development models that teach people living in poverty, illness, or post-conflict or disaster situations how to help themselves. Yes, you can still sit alongside dying people in the hospitals and cry with children who've lost their mothers. Perhaps some Bleeding Hearts will live in the slums, becoming part of a poor community. But seek to recruit a team that includes other types of teammates to complement you and encourage you.

The Strategic Thinker

"I'm motivated by the numbers," a Strategic Thinker says with logic and passion. This person remembers that six thousand unreached people groups are left in the world. About half of them are unengaged, and therefore, no cross-cultural workers are even trying to live among them. A Strategic Thinker recalls that there are only five cross-cultural workers going to every one million Hindus; meanwhile, there are seven hundred workers for every million people that already call themselves Christian (chapter 6).

Numbers like these stir Strategic Thinkers to action, urging them to logically assess and solve the dire imbalance. The lack of resources and the effort that remains to be put forth disturbs Strategic Thinkers. They conclude that more people need to cross cultures and be catalysts for the good news in places that are unreached and unengaged by the gospel.

As a Strategic Thinker, you might incorrectly assume you wouldn't be the one to actually go overseas, because you aren't a Bleeding Heart—the kind you often perceive as the right type of overseas workers. But ascribing to this traditional view clouds your perception of how your specific personality could supercharge work in another country. Strategic Thinkers, as voices of logic and productivity, provide necessary big-picture thinking. You efficiently run organizations, as well as develop and promote strategies that lead to fruitfulness.

David Watson, who cowrote *Contagious Disciple Making: Leading Others on a Journey of Discovery*, is an example of a Strategic Thinker who stayed awake at night thinking about how planting one church in his lifetime wouldn't saturate the unreached people group where he lived. He envisioned the big picture, the end goal, and experimented with steps to get there. God blessed Watson's strategic thinking to catalyze more than seventy movements to Christ globally, resulting in almost a hundred thousand new churches.[3]

Most strategic thinkers are already ambitious and driven in their areas of expertise. You are probably busy, so pausing in your pursuits long enough to consider the state of the world—and your role in it—proves challenging. Your logical thinking and busy schedule makes it easy for you to dismiss global nudges that might cause you to pause and ask, "Does it make sense for *me* to move overseas long-term?" This leaves overseas ministries short of this type of men and women like you.

If you are a Strategic Thinker, know that we need you to consider bringing your God-given personality with you overseas to places where Jesus isn't known and no one is going. Just think about it.

The Adventure Seeker

More times than I can count, I've heard someone say, "I really like to travel. If I moved overseas, or joined a short-term trip, it would be for selfish reasons. It can't be God telling me to go, because I would just really love it!"

Can I just say to you, the Adventure Seeker—you who love to try new foods and talk to strange people, who get all buzzy inside when an airplane flies overhead, dreaming of beaches in Tahiti, climbing the Himalayas, or hanging out the back of a jeep on a jungle safari—you were made to live in another culture. And you can redeem this desire by doing it for God's glory.

"There are men for whom the unattainable has a special attraction. Usually they are not experts: their ambitions and fantasies are strong enough to brush aside the doubts which more cautious men might have. Determination and faith are their strongest weapons. At best such men are regarded as eccentric; at worst, mad," pronounced Walt Unsworth, who made it to the top of Mount Everest.[4]

Don't let the thought that moving overseas might be fun stop you from considering this career for your life. Sometimes Adventure Seekers are so busy planning vacations or safaris or treks up the Himalayas that they miss the opportunity to consider adventuring overseas for a spiritual purpose. Don't dismiss this God-given desire—to experience life in all its variety—as an unspiritual drive. Don't relegate this thirst for adventure to mere pleasure or a $5,000 splurge on a two-week trip rafting the Amazon.

I loved studying French all four years of high school and would dream of visiting Paris and the Eiffel Tower and perhaps falling in love alongside the river Seine. On occasion, I still spend the evening researching European countries, plotting out a summer adventure through Germany and Austria, and could I squeeze in another few days if I rented a car and drove through Italy?

Whenever I plan a short-term trip for work to visit field workers or to survey a city where no workers live, I look for a long layover in another country I've never been to, so I can say I've been there. God put this inside of me! I actually pray for God to bring to life my love for travel, experiences, and other cultures as I traverse the world in his name.

Give yourself permission to consider a career overseas that you might really love and to have fun doing. This also has great eternal significance. Yes, there will be suffering. It will be hard. But for now, know that the lure of adventure is something God put inside of you.

The Obedient Disciple

Obedient Disciples consider moving overseas as emissaries for Jesus, because it's the right thing to do. They take Jesus' words to go into all the world seriously. They feel most fulfilled, and closest to God, when they obey and do things they believe they should do. From my untested view, about a third of global workers that I've met fall into this category. Compelled by duty and responsibility, they often speak with words such as "should" and "ought to." Obedient Disciples convincingly affirm, "It's our responsibility to go into all the world."

Sometimes Obedient Disciples get sidetracked from considering work overseas because of responsibilities to provide for their families. You may be more concerned with safety than other types and more cautious about doing activities you perceive as crazy, roll-the-dice, or irresponsible—like putting your family in danger or "throwing away" the security of your career.

I say to you, the Obedient Disciples, revise your concept of responsibility so that it first aligns with God's purposes and priorities. We *need* you, the Obedient Disciples, to consider overseas roles, because you can persevere. Once your minds and hearts embrace the task of being cross-cultural catalysts for peace with God, your deep sense of obedience and duty will sustain you, longer than most, through difficult situations overseas.

The Meaning and Purpose Person

"I want to make a difference in the world!" announces the person motivated by meaning and purpose. It's easy to ask these types to consider a career overseas for the glory of God. Their internal engines roar to life when inspired by the promise of deeper influence and significance. The prospect of influencing even one person, and more so thousands, engages Meaning and Purpose people to consider overseas work. After all, they would throw themselves into selling nuts and bolts if it meant that it might result in a rocket spaceship that would find a new planet on which to broadcast back a save-the-world message.

The humanly impossible task of catalyzing thousands of people toward Jesus, in a language you've never spoken in a culture you don't know, doesn't deter you, the Meaning and Purpose person. As long as the vision toward purpose is clear, you consider the task a possibility.

As a Meaning and Purpose person, you will flourish when you meet other Meaning and Purpose people, and many kindred spirits will you meet overseas. If you find that people in your home country don't always understand your intrinsic motivation, your intuition, and your depth of soul, you will likely find yourself in like-minded company with other field workers when you move overseas. You will just "know" each other, and your soul will feel as though it's found its community.

The Disciples' Transformation . . . and Yours Too

What motivates ordinary followers of Jesus with varying personalities, who are pursuing careers, family, and comfortable lives, to care about people in other cultures? What motivates you? Why are a growing number of believers exchanging the American dream for a role in giving all nations access to the kingdom of God? The same things that motivated eleven home-grown, ordinary men—a few fishermen, businessmen, and a doctor—to care about people of other cultures, even choosing death by martyrdom in foreign lands. They encountered Jesus. Transformation occurred in Jesus' original disciples' hearts and minds as they spent time with and grew closer to their Rabbi, moving them from fishermen to fishers of men, aligning them with God's vision to reach the entire world. Let's take a closer look at the steps to transformation.

First, the disciples followed Jesus. They followed him and obeyed him, doing what he did, loving as he loved. They saw how God meant for the world to be. They watched Jesus heal the sick, raise the dead, and cast out demons. In their presence, he empowered women, denounced religious hypocrisy, and welcomed children. They heard Jesus teach truth, forgive sins, elevate the poor, and love his enemies. They saw the King of the kingdom of God in action and learned to do likewise.

You can do this too. Follow Jesus.

Second, the disciples caught his teaching that good news should be shared with others, even those in other cultures. Jesus took the long way around and chose an unscheduled stop when he walked from Judea to Galilee one day. He invited his disciples on a short-term experience through Samaria and demonstrated God's heart for people from different cultures. He gave good news to a disregarded Samaritan woman, who shared it with her

> TRANSFORMATION OCCURRED IN JESUS' ORIGINAL DISCIPLES' HEARTS AND MINDS AS THEY SPENT TIME WITH AND GREW CLOSER TO THEIR RABBI, MOVING THEM FROM FISHERMEN TO FISHERS OF MEN.

village, and many came to follow Jesus as the Messiah (John 4:1–43). Jesus thrust his reluctant disciples into uncomfortable, innovative ways of interacting with society—and the rest of the world—and showed them what could happen.

Another time, Jesus announced to his disciples, "Let's go to the Decapolis!" He surprised his probably hesitant Jewish disciples with a trip across the lake to this non-Jewish area of ten Greek cities, the home of a foreign, pagan nation. On the other side, Jesus freed a demon-possessed man from a legion of spirits and ordered them into a herd of pigs, which all dove off a cliff to their demise in the sea below. He sent the transformed man back to his own people in the Greek cities to show them the new life that Jesus had created for the man, by the power of God (Mark 4:35–5:20).

You can do this too. Share good news with others.

Third, the disciples caught Jesus' vision for the future that included all nations. Jesus' words motivate believers even today, waiting for his return: "And the Good News about the Kingdom will be preached throughout the whole world, so that all the nations will hear it; and then the end will come (Matt. 24:14).

Even though the gospel stories are primarily set in the Jewish region, the disciples consistently watched Jesus dismantle the boundaries of his current Jewish culture to include Gentiles in his plan. On one of his repeat visits to the region of Tyre and Sidon, a primarily Greek region, he answered the plea of a Canaanite woman begging for him to cast out a demon from her daughter.

After responding the way his disciples might have responded, saying that only the Jews deserve his mercy, he turned full circle and said, "Woman, you have great faith! Your request is granted." And he healed her daughter at that moment (Matt. 15:28). His actions hinted at the future massive inclusion of Gentiles in the promises of God.

You can do this too. Catch God's vision for the future of all nations worshiping him.

The disciples' transformation started with saying yes to Jesus over and over. New experiences led to a new mind-set, which led to new ways of practicing their daily lives under the guidance of Jesus. As they followed and obeyed Jesus more and more, deeper and deeper, they fell captive to God's heart to find the lost sheep (Luke 15:3–7), to search for the lost coin (Luke 15:8–10), to gather those not originally invited to the kingdom feast (Luke 14:15–24), and to answer the plea of the Roman centurion (Matt. 8:5–13).

And then, finally, to complete their transformation, God's Spirit invaded their very souls and made them new. Because of all of this, their affections widened, desiring people from every background, every nation, to worship the one true God and embrace his plan for reconciliation to himself.

After three years of mind-and perspective-stretching experiences with Jesus, his disciples watched him die and rise again, and they experienced the Spirit of God come in his place at Pentecost, where "God-fearing Jews from every nation under heaven" were present (Acts 2:1–11).

Then, we finally find the disciples chasing after God's heart for the nations.

God gave Peter a significant cross-cultural assignment in his present context, which likely freed others also to invite other cultures into God's redemptive plan. Repeated visions from God nudged Peter to accept an invitation from the Gentile officer Cornelius, breaking Jewish tradition to enter the home of a Gentile. Cornelius, a God-fearing, influential man in his city, and his entire family, came to faith in Jesus that day (Acts 10:1–48).

While scripture doesn't inform us, legend and history books indicate that most of the disciples traveled all over the inhabited world. Christians in what is now Russia claim Andrew as the first to bring the gospel to their land, and he also traveled to Asia Minor, modern-day Turkey, and Greece, where he met his end by crucifixion.

Christians in southern India credit Thomas as their founder. Philip possibly had a ministry in North Africa and Asia Minor. Matthew, the tax collector and writer of one of the Gospels, was believed to have preached in Ethiopia, and in Persia, along with Simon the Zealot. It's believed that Bartholomew traveled with Thomas to India, and also to Ethiopia and southern Arabia. It's recorded that James worked in Syria, as did Matthias, alongside Andrew.[5]

How did this all happen? Their hearts started to beat as God's heart beats, and they realized they could follow Jesus to the nations in their neighborhood . . . and beyond. It changed the way they lived their lives. It didn't happen overnight, but it did happen.

And it can happen to you.

Reflection

1. What expectations have you placed on yourself to already fit the skills and description of a gifted overseas field worker? How can you release them to God?
2. What expectations do you have for God to supernaturally confirm an overseas calling, even before you take a few steps in that direction? How can you take a few small steps of saying yes?
3. What personality description fits you most: Bleeding Heart, a Strategic Thinker, an Adventure Seeker, an Obedient Disciple, or a Meaning and Purpose person? Who are friends in your life that fit one of these descriptions who might come with you if you asked them?

TEN

Dreaming About Overseas Professions and Earthly Impact

Now that we've started to dream about moving to live around the world, we might wonder what it practically looks like to live overseas. How do we get into a country? What would we do there? Who would we be there? What kind of specific earthly impact in causes such as poverty alleviation, education, or social justice could we make? And how do disciple making, church planting, running a business overseas, and affecting social change all fit together?

Even if we don't go overseas ourselves, understanding the answers to these questions will position us to advocate, support, and pray for those who do go, so it's worth us taking the time to explore the answers to these questions about potential overseas roles.

God is often pleased to use our life experiences, education, and personal passions as part of our official identity in a country overseas. This might come as a relief, even a surprise, if we imagine being a field worker can only involve building a hut in a jungle somewhere in Africa. The landscape of the unreached world is different today than it was fifty years ago. Many populations and family members from unreached people groups have migrated to urban centers. Few people groups remain isolated in remote jungles and villages. And because much of the time the countries we'll need to enter rarely give out religious worker visas, it's helpful, even necessary, to make use of the skills we already possess.

Yes, our primary purpose is still to introduce Jesus Christ to those without access to his good news. But be prepared to have another official identity in your adopted country, which will most likely be different from—but complementary to—your primary purpose. Your official identity is authentic. It's not fake. Your identity as a businessperson, a development worker, or a student is who you really are and what you really do during your working hours. And that identity will truly bless communities and families. We can fashion our identities in ways that allow us the best chance of catalyzing a movement to Jesus Christ.

Much of the time, countries where the largest concentrations of unreached people groups live are not political allies with Western countries. This means, as Westerners, we can't just go in and out of the country as if we were a Canadian crossing the border into America with a passport in hand. For example, Westerners traveling to Pakistan, Algeria, or the Russian Caucasus must apply for long-term visas that show a valid reason for living in the country.

Field workers who enter and live in majority Hindu, Muslim, Buddhist, or formerly Communist countries can adopt one of the following five identities: a business entrepreneur, a community development practitioner, a student, an employee at an international company, or, in a few places, a religious worker. We won't discuss identities you might adopt in a country with a significant Christian population. Instead, let's focus in on the identities most helpful to entering the places where few, if any, Christian communities exist and where the majority of unreached people groups live.

You may be a college student, a young couple, or a single. You may be in your middle years, with children in school, or you may even be retired. Keep an open mind as you imagine yourself in one of these identities living overseas.

Business Entrepreneur

The government of a country, like Indonesia, can grant business visas to legitimate businesspeople from a foreign country, like Canada. Here's how it worked for Doug, a banker from Canada. Pursuing God's heart for the nations, he began to pray for the Sunda people group in Indonesia. Doug applied with an international agency that sends field workers to where the Sunda lived. As he completed the agency's candidate process to prepare to live overseas, he started his own financial consulting company in Canada and incorporated as a business. Joining networks that promoted Business as Mission (BAM) and Business for Transformation (B4T) grew his learning and helped him dream.[1]

On a short-term survey trip to the island of Java, he met with a family from his agency living there, and they invited him to join them for a longer time. A believing Indonesian businessman he connected with agreed to write a letter of invitation for Doug to start a business in Indonesia, assuring the Indonesian consulate that he would take responsibility for this foreigner.

Doug also wrote a letter to the Indonesian consulate, asking for permission to open a branch of his Canadian business in Indonesia. He filled out an application for a business visa, included the inviting letter and the sending letter, and mailed them to the consulate.

A month later, he received his passport, stamped with a business visa that allowed him to be in the country for a set length of time.

He raised financial support from family, friends, and businesses—including business start-up costs. Doug's church and the sending agency commissioned him to share the gospel as a businessman to the Sunda, and he flew to East Java in Indonesia to join his team. Right away, Doug joined an intensive, full-time language program while researching options on the kind of businesses that could bless Sunda families.

What kinds of businesses work well overseas?

Service-based businesses, such as language centers, tourism agencies, or education centers, work well in foreign countries. A business could distribute a product made in the country or provide training on a needed job skill. Service-based businesses (run by field workers trying to bless communities with the gospel) strive to be profitable enough to pay for operating expenses and salaries for local employees. But rarely can a service-based business fully support a Westerner's salary.

Other field workers try to start manufacturing companies, although it takes expertise and more financial capital to make them profitable. Oliver runs a profitable company that designs and manufactures products used in disaster situations. His company builds the product in-country using local resources and labor, but several field workers with degrees in engineering also work for the company. They sell to local nongovernment organizations (NGOs), so the product comes from the local population (and not a foreign entity) during relief situations, such as recovery efforts following flooding, typhoons, or earthquakes.

Having done business in the city for years, Oliver has built an honorable reputation for operating his company with integrity. He sells high-quality products at fair prices with exemplary customer service. His business also creates jobs and provides employees with enough income to support dozens of families.

The city leaders recognize him as a man who contributes to their community, worships the one true God, and follows the ways of Jesus. They know he operates his business on biblical principles, never offering bribes, which is customary in the culture. His friends and employees come to him for prayer, conflict management, and advice, and he shares about Jesus in practical ways relevant to their everyday lives.

"I know all the influential people in this city," Oliver said when I interviewed him about his work. He pointed to a few plates and cups on a table in front of him and continued, "It's like the table is set."

Holding a teacup, he smiled and, in his thick Australian accent, said, "This is the grandmother. With each interaction, God is moving her a little to the right. This plate is the uncle, and God has moved him too. I'm waiting for the time when the Holy Spirit suddenly pulls the tablecloth out from under all of them. It will happen when they are all ready to follow Jesus at one time. So that they can all come to faith together in one motion as a community. The tablecloth—their dependence on their own good works—will be gone, and they will all be close to the table, Jesus, but still in their own community."

Some business owners operate as social entrepreneurs, running businesses for profit but with an eye to create social and community change or to lift people out of poverty. Terra's company runs an assessment center for blind children. Located on the outskirts of a slum in a one-room clinic, Terra hired local optometrists to examine the children. She's recruited a couple and another single woman from her home country to join her in her business and kingdom work. Believing staff members spend most of their time training parents whose children test as blind. Meeting in families' homes, Terra's staff teaches braille to the children and train parents to help their children live productive lives.

Terra's business charges a small fee for the assessments and training—enough to cover the costs of local employees and building overhead. At the same time, it's a form of social work, because her business addresses a felt need for those living in poverty. Putting it all together, her business meets a need in the community, provides a valid identity in a place where foreigners don't normally go, and gives her and her employees access to families in order to search for people of peace with whom to share Jesus.

Another relatively new idea among business-minded field workers is to *only* start the kinds of businesses that could lead to a movement of people coming to Jesus Christ. William is a former business consultant for Fortune 500 companies in America. Today, he helps field workers start businesses compatible with disciple-making movement strategies.

"Businesses that lead to movements should have low operating costs, be service-based, and create access to many people in order to find people of peace," William advises. "They should bless whole families and communities and also allow time for the owner to engage in relationships."

William coaches field workers to apply the traditional advice for doing solid business overseas: start a business that makes sense to the local population, plan to be profitable, and make your identity credible and valid in order to gain honor in the city. William also encourages business owners to be spiritually conspicuous from the beginning, making it known that they are followers of God and will run their businesses in ways that are pleasing and honorable to him.

Sometimes the very idea of starting a business can feel overwhelming. Few field workers have business backgrounds or experience launching businesses as entrepreneurs. It's difficult enough to start a business in our home country, where we know the language and culture. Add the complexities of a foreign language and business culture to the stress and shock of entering a new country, and the chances of business success are quite small.

YOU *CAN* SUCCEED IN BUSINESS AND SPIRITUAL GOALS IF YOU SHOW HUMILITY IN WHATEVER YOU DO AND WHEREVER YOU GO, AN EAGERNESS TO LEARN FROM OTHERS, AND A STRONG WORK ETHIC.

However, most organizations sending field workers overseas now offer business coaching, apprenticeships, and franchising of existing kingdom businesses. Be encouraged that you *can* succeed in business and spiritual goals if you show humility in whatever you do and wherever you go, an eagerness to learn from others, and a strong work ethic.

William and other business owners suggest entering a larger city first, to learn language and culture. While gaining fluency in the language, entrepreneurs can experiment by taking small steps, trying one thing, then another, to see which business ideas might work before moving to work in an area where fewer Westerners live.

Nongovernmental Organization (NGO) Development Worker

Starting or working for nongovernmental organizations, or NGOs, is another option for entering a foreign country on a valid visa. If you have a heart to walk alongside people living in poverty or crisis, you might consider a cross-cultural career working with an NGO. An NGO is not run by the government but by private, not-for-profit parties wanting to do good in a community. An NGO can be faith-based or secular. But most do run on principles compatible with the Judeo-Christian value of "love your neighbor as yourself" (Matt. 22:39).

Lucas and Mia both received their undergraduate degrees from a secular university in community development with a minor in international affairs. They completed a practicum internship with a faith-based NGO in Asia, empowering women in rural Asian communities. When they graduated, they negotiated with the NGO to spend six months in full-time language learning in a rural village. These organizations are often short on employees, so allowing time to focus on language isn't common. But they stuck to their ideals and made sure to get the dedicated time right in the beginning.

As Lucas and Mia grew in language ability and culture acquisition, they started to work alongside the two hundred local employees. They moved to the main city, where they now train and coach local employees on healthy community development practices at the headquarters and provide a link back to their home country's main office.

Their organization oversees community development work in more than seven hundred rural villages in one of the poorest countries in the world using an empowering model. Local employees build relationships in the village and gather local leaders, helping them identify women living in poverty who show motivation, potential, and need. These women organize into small groups of ten to fifteen that meet daily to start literacy classes. They learn how to read and write, save money, and start businesses, and they also learn their legal rights—all from a biblical worldview.

Women's groups start collective savings accounts to jump-start their own businesses, such as chicken farms, goat milk distribution, or tailoring. Literacy helps them manage and grow their businesses and gives them the confidence and desire to invest in their children's futures by enrolling them in schools. Knowledge of the law empowers the women to stand up for their rights—such as refusing to allow their preteen girls to be married off as child brides. Lucas and Mia disciple interested local employees into the kingdom of God, and teach them to do the same with the women they coach.

Working for an NGO can be rewarding, as it is for Lucas and Mia, but it's also easy to drown in the dire physical needs of the people being served—and to lose sight of introducing people to Jesus Christ. If you are intent on spiritually impacting unreached people groups and you decide to join or start an NGO, link arms with a sending organization intent on disciple making so you stay intentional about spiritual goals.

Some NGO leaders may discourage you from engaging in spiritual conversations for fear of losing the privilege to operate in the country. If you do your research and ask good questions regarding these issues, you can find and join effective NGOs doing holistic work in spiritually strategic countries.

Student

Foreigners can also enter other countries on student visas. Local universities accept foreigners into degree programs to study the trade language of the country or a specific area of interest. Entering on a student visa provides a valid reason to be studying language full-time—and you also earn a degree in the language.

Julio and Maria, citizens of Brazil, chose to study English as well as the trade language at a local university in a major city overseas. A field worker already on the ground filled out reams of paperwork to help them get an invitation from the university to study. Because not many Brazilian field workers live in this country halfway across the world, living on a student visa allowed them several years to explore longer-term options for Brazilians, and other Ibero-Americans, to enter and stay in this country.

One challenge with student visas is that they have a limited lifetime. Field workers can't be students forever, and they don't want to be known in a country as permanent students. Furthermore, the locals could perceive students as transient, limiting access to the people group they are trying to reach. However, three to four years as a student in a country gives ample time to explore other options for establishing a more permanent identity in the country.

Professional

In some countries, like Saudi Arabia, the preferred visa option for Westerners is employment at an international company located inside its borders. Major corporations in industries such as medicine, aerospace, information technology, automotive, and textiles run offices in countries that are spiritually strategic.

The world is getting smaller. Visit just about any large city in a country halfway around the world from the United States, and you'll encounter Colonel Sanders and KFC, Baskin-Robbins, Starbucks, McDonald's, Coke, and Pepsi, all capitalizing on the global market. Why not work for one of them? They'll pay you. You'll get a visa. And you'll live in countries with massive populations of unreached people groups.

William Carey lived in India in the 1800s, translating portions of the Bible into more than forty languages. His salary as a part-time university professor helped fund his translation work and supplemented his income from his mission board. He also founded other colleges and educational institutions in the country as a business.

Though the lure of a steady income, the ability to use your skills, and arriving with the backing of an international company are strong, few field workers tend to go this route and usually try to find another way to enter. A lot of times this is because leadership careers in international corporations and businesses require more than forty hours a week. Finding the time to search for people of peace, start home fellowships, or coach and disciple those coming to faith can easily take second place to finishing a presentation for your employer's board meeting. Your employer will expect you to start working as soon as you land in-country, leaving little time to learn the language. Also, you may not be working directly with the unreached population God calls you to reach.

But in countries where entering as an employee of a corporation is the only option, a family calling will be important, and spouses can work in partnership to disciple people. As a professional, you can also be strategic by intentionally investing your time and consolidating your sphere of influence in your workplace, as discussed in chapter 2.

Also, if you already work for a company with an international branch and you are simply willing to change locations, consider accepting an international job transfer to a strategic location. If you do this, align yourself with a sending organization so you can fellowship with other field workers there, learn practical discipleship methods, and be encouraged to integrate your faith and work.

Religious Worker

Though rare, some countries in unreached parts of the world offer limited supplies of visas for religious workers. These visas used to be the main way that field workers entered countries. They came as missionaries, they identified as missionaries, and they openly practiced as missionaries. They started Christian schools, hospitals, Bible schools, and churches. Trained linguists entered tribal areas to document unwritten languages, teach literacy, translate the Bible, and lead chronological Bible studies.

While uncommon, a few majority Muslim or Buddhist countries, for example, still do allow local churches and nonprofit charities to sponsor a number of foreigners on religious worker visas. Field workers who choose this identity and are granted a visa usually work closely under the supervision of a local religious nonprofit.

It may seem remarkable to get into a "closed" country in such an open way. But the catch is that proselytizing or encouraging someone to change his or her religion is illegal in most of these countries. While you may be interested in introducing someone to Jesus Christ, and not Western Christianity per se, the government won't believe that. You may be allowed to teach other believers, but the government will watch you closely in your interactions with people who don't identify as Christian.

The most strategic work for those entering on religious visas is to concentrate on catalyzing existing believers to reach out to nearby people groups that have not had a chance to hear about and respond to Jesus Christ.

TRAITS OF IDENTITIES COMPATIBLE WITH DISCIPLE-MAKING MOVEMENTS

Whichever identity you embrace in a foreign country, consider one that's compatible with starting a movement of people to Jesus. Compare the characteristics of your entry options to this list:

- Allows you to live legitimately in the country
- Gives you a respectable, honorable, and credible identity in the country
- Gives you access to many people in order to find men and women of peace

- Gives you access to members of the people group you're trying to reach
- Blesses families and communities
- Gives you relational time with the people you're trying to reach
- Allows time for making disciples

Church-Planting, Poverty Alleviation, and Social Justice (Or All Three?)

In business, development, student, professional, and religious worker identities, activities such as church planting, training nationals, business as mission, microfinance, community development, relief efforts, education, social justice, clean water delivery, disease eradication, poverty alleviation, and Bible translation all compete for prominence. Which of these activities are best to focus on? How do they interact with one another? And how do they interact with the five identities just named?

#1: Church Planting

Church planters living in unreached people groups pray for multiple, replicating, indigenous house church fellowships. Remember: the church planter is also a businessperson, a development worker, a student, a professional, or perhaps a religious worker. Church planters pray for disciple-making movements (DMM), also known as church-planting movements (CPM), involving thousands of people embracing Christ (chapter 5). Such movements launch into uncontrollable, uncountable forward trajectory, with entire communities coming to faith.

Field workers like Danny, who led Adam to Christ (the one who washed dishes for his wife in chapter 4), make it their primary task to start fellowships of Jesus followers that start other fellowships of Jesus followers. Danny keeps a list of the local people he's discipling. He meets with them several times a week to study scripture together, practice obeying it, and pray. He texts them, exercises with them, eats with them, and works with them in his business during the day.

They interact constantly, and as Danny coaches and disciples them, they learn and grow more like Jesus. Danny intentionally encourages specific Christlike attributes and tries to instill certain principles. One of those characteristics is to disciple others and to teach their disciples how to disciple others.

Danny and Adam keep a private list of their disciples, and their disciples' disciples. They keep a record of discovery Bible studies that start in people's homes, how many are coming regularly, how many are baptized, and who is coaching whom. There are symbols next to names and groups indicating baptisms, scripture study groups, and potential new leaders. Danny and Adam regularly update and pray over the names on this drawing board. Danny also wakes early to spend time with Jesus, getting daily direction and encouragement from God on his plans.

Some field workers still take a traditional approach of planting one church with a building and putting a denominational name on the front. This strategy reflects the accepted form of church in Westernized countries. However, church planters working with the least-reached peoples agree that this approach is neither sustainable nor reproducible enough to plant the gospel wide enough—so that churches can continue multiplying on their own. It would take hundreds of years to saturate an unreached people group with this approach. Instead, church-planting movement approaches help people discover Jesus Christ, as they obey God by studying the Bible together in small groups meeting in homes.[2] Facilitated by a respected member of a family line who is being coached outside the group, without any financial overhead, denominational affiliation, or paid staff, the home groups can more quickly reproduce.

CPM and DMM practitioners adopt roles as *catalyst trainers*. While they reach out to a specific people group, they also train local believers in movement principles and discipleship. In doing so, church planters increase their effectiveness exponentially by coaching and mentoring local believers, who have more language and cultural insight—and who often see fruit faster.

Danny moved into a catalyst role after Adam came to faith and started winning others to Jesus and forming house churches. By God's favor, the movement is replicating quickly so that, in only a couple of years, eight different family lines, each replicating four generations deep, continue to multiply. Danny coaches Adam, who coaches disciples leading their clans, who disciple their disciples.

As David Garrison wrote in *Church Planting Movements: How God is Redeeming a Lost World*, "Church Planting Movements are simply a way that God is drawing massive numbers of lost persons into saving community with himself. That saving relationship—rather than any movement or method—is what touches the end vision, the glory of God, that we so desire."[3]

#2: Poverty Alleviation

In recent years, Western churches have grown more aware of and more bothered by pandemic poverty issues, such as lack of clean water, hunger, malaria, AIDS, and illiteracy. But if we want to impact a materially poor community, we must first get knowledgeable about it! History shows that it's too easy to do more harm than good when attempting to alleviate poverty in foreign cultures. Not all types of poverty—or approaches to poverty alleviation—are created equal.

"A helpful first step in thinking about working with the poor in any context is to discern whether the situation calls for relief, rehabilitation or development," wrote poverty alleviation experts Steve Corbett and Brian Fikkert in *When Helping Hurts: How to Alleviate Poverty Without Hurting the Poor and Yourself.* "In fact, the failure to distinguish among these situations is one of the most common reasons that poverty-alleviation efforts do harm."[4] Let's take a moment to look at the difference between the three.

NOT ALL TYPES OF POVERTY—OR APPROACHES TO POVERTY ALLEVIATION— ARE CREATED EQUAL.

Relief work "stops the bleeding" following disasters such as tsunamis, hurricanes, earthquakes, and floods. The good Samaritan story is a good example of a relief effort done well (Luke 10:25–37). The Samaritan bandaged the dying man's wounds, brought him to a hospital, and immediately stopped the bleeding in a situation where the man could not help himself.

Once the bleeding stopped, a second stage, of *rehabilitation*, began, in which the helper worked alongside the hurting to rebuild what was lost.

The third stage of poverty alleviation is called *development*. "This is a "process of ongoing change that moves all the people involved—both the 'helpers' and the 'helped'—closer to being in right relationship with God, others and creation. In particular, as the materially poor develop, they are better able to fulfill their calling of glorifying God by working and supporting themselves and their families with the fruits of their labor,"[5] wrote Corbett and Fikkert.

Liz, a pediatrician from Michigan, left her medical practice in America to work in preventative health care in developing countries. She moved to a country in Africa, learned the language, and started visiting people living in rural villages.

She saw how more babies died than lived. Diseases and preventable complications from illnesses such as diarrhea regularly killed small children. So she met with community leaders in a village, gained their trust, and asked if they would form a group to address what they felt were the community's most dire needs. She helped facilitate this group as they identified the strengths and capabilities they held in their hands—their assets—to find out how they could help their families and children thrive.

Without using any outside funding, Liz first empowered the community leaders to adopt a new worldview through her training, one that led them out of a poverty mind-set and into a biblical mind-set, affirming how God values them. After this, they identified ways to address infant mortality together. Then the community leaders themselves walked from house to house, telling simple stories with pictures to educate mothers on solutions. The picture stories also related to a story from the Bible. For example, while teaching someone the importance of handwashing, the picture card included prompts for the verse about how God can "Purify me from my sins, and I will be clean; wash me, and I will be whiter than snow" (Ps. 51:7).

Development usually requires a community effort to address root causes and to empower entire groups. Faith-based poverty alleviation efforts include a spiritual component that aims to reconcile individuals and communities to God. These efforts may also bring in elements of microfinance and group savings, both of which incorporate business and moral principles. Community Health Education (CHE) is the method that Liz used. It combines preventative medicine, asset-based training, and Bible storying.[6]

Educational programs in community development often involve sponsoring children from impoverished families so they can attend school. In these programs, it's important to work closely with family members to provide well-rounded solutions to improve the overall quality of life in the household. Successful development programs are often holistic, addressing multiple facets of poverty.

#3: Social Justice

We long for the day when everything will be made right. It's sickening to read of the injustices of children sold into slavery on the border of Nepal; and minorities slaughtered in cold blood in Nigeria, Uganda, and Syria. My blood boils when I hear of children rolling cigarettes in Cairo twelve hours a day, women on sale for prostitution in Bangkok, and poor people imprisoned unjustly in India for the inability to pay a bribe. We cry out to God for justice and say, "When will you avenge the evil?!"

Until recently, the conservative evangelical community in the West regarded social activists as liberal—and even questioned the depth of their spirituality. That's changing, though. The church is getting involved in fighting for the rights of the oppressed, albeit slowly and without much experience in protesting social injustice.

The United Nations defined social justice as "an underlying principle for peaceful and prosperous coexistence within and among nations. We uphold the principles of social justice when we promote gender equality or the rights of indigenous peoples and migrants. We advance social justice when we remove barriers that people face because of gender, age, race, ethnicity, religion, culture or disability.

"For the United Nations," the website continues, "the pursuit of social justice for all is at the core of our global mission to promote development and human dignity."[7]

Because social justice is a fairly new arena for the average North American churchgoer, our first step is to bravely recognize the complexity of justice issues. We must also be willing to bring both disciple making and poverty alleviation into the efforts to address social injustices.

Michael is an attorney working in a country known for its open brothels and child slavery. A faith-based nonprofit justice mission holds a license to advise local attorneys in prosecution cases. He, along with other employees, works with local law enforcement and justice nonprofits to prosecute the bouncers and pimps behind the illegal industry of sex trafficking.

It's arduous work, with deep, systemic issues involving the reasons for the illegal trade itself; the worldview of the local people, which asserts that a person is born into her situation and cannot change it; and the government corruption complicating every case. But like William Carey in his decades-long fight against *sati*, the practice of widow burning, they persevere, fighting to see the kingdom come on earth as it is in heaven.

Michael's wife manages the office of a small faith-based rehabilitation home in a hill station far away from the chaos. The social service branch of the government sends minors rescued from trafficking to the home for rehabilitation and job training. It's a long road of healing, but with Jesus Christ the Healer, and an on-staff psychologist, child-development specialists, and even an art therapist who visits occasionally, the girls sent to the rehabilitation home walk the long road toward true freedom.

How the Kingdom of God Creates Social Change

Social injustice is often tied to the same issues that cause systemic material poverty—and to a damaged worldview not based on the Bible. In any of the five identities for living overseas to make disciples, we will have the opportunity to create positive change within a society.

For example, if you work for a community development organization, by teaching women to read and write, you're combating social injustice. If a woman in Niger cannot read because she lives in a slum, then she cannot know the law to stand up for her rights. Her daughters could be sold as slaves to pay a debt she owes, and she is not equipped to stop it. Human rights organization UNESCO says the right to be literate is essential "for eradicating poverty, reducing child mortality, curbing population growth, achieving gender equality and ensuring sustainable development, peace and democracy."[8] Further, literacy levels also relate somewhat to a country's level of exposure to Jesus. The five countries with the highest populations of illiterate women (India, Pakistan, Nigeria, Ethiopia, and Bangladesh) also contain some of the highest populations of unreached people groups.[9]

Injustice rears its ugly head wherever the light of Jesus does not shine so bright. If you live as a businessperson focused on a church-planting movement, you will combat social injustice. True freedom in social arenas only comes when people operate under the reign and rule of God, in the way he intended. If communities of new believers regularly meet to worship God, hold each other accountable, and read and obey scripture, we pray they would also have courage to stand up and shout out that women should not be sold as slaves, minorities should not be attacked, refugees should not be abandoned, and unborn babies should not be killed.

That sounds like America, doesn't it? Yes, racial and sexual discrimination is still graphically rearing its ugly head in America, which has a constitution written by men who held a biblical worldview. And yes, trafficking occurs on Western soil, too. However, mass graves aren't being dug by a dictator who murders his own citizens in a rage, as in North Korea. Girls aren't being sold by the thousands in an open slave market on the border, as in Nepal. And 80 percent of the population is not illiterate or starving, as in Yemen.

If the kingdom of God, the way God intends for the world to be, comes to a people group, women will start to be valued, the wealthy will begin to share with the poor, orphans will be brought into homes, and the peace Jesus Christ offers will stem hatred, fighting, and war. While evil will war against good until Jesus returns, communities of people following the ways of Jesus can influence the fabric of entire countries.

As you imagine the possibilities for a Christ follower living in another country, you can see that an identity will hold elements of several different aspects you've read in this chapter. Someone living in another country may start house fellowships, disciple believers, run a business, be involved in a charity, help lift families out of poverty, or fight a social injustice at different times and seasons in a career overseas. God may be asking you to humbly and creatively consider investing your life and profession for his purposes in another nation.

WHILE EVIL WILL WAR AGAINST GOOD UNTIL JESUS RETURNS, COMMUNITIES OF PEOPLE FOLLOWING THE WAYS OF JESUS CAN INFLUENCE THE FABRIC OF ENTIRE COUNTRIES.

Reflection

1. Which identity for full-time overseas work—a businessperson, community development worker, student, or religious worker—intrigues you or makes the most sense to you, and why?
2. What would keep you from considering one of these identities as an option for yourself? Write them down and keep them in mind as you read the last chapters.
3. Which areas of global work spoke to your heart, mind, and soul: church planting, poverty alleviation, or social injustice, or a combination? Why? How could you take a step toward doing something about it?

ELEVEN

Surrendering the American Dream

"Why? Why, why, WHY would you move to India, when you have everything here in America?" an Iraqi boy in eighth grade said as he gestured around our beautiful suburban home in genuine disbelief. "You have a good job. It's safe here. It's the dream for everyone to come to America! Why would you leave?!"

I stumbled over my answer. His passionate disbelief that we would relinquish such wealth and comfort for anything less caught me off guard. I knew he also spoke from the pain and experience of having once lost security and normalcy in his own life.

Jesus told of a certain successful businessman whose life breathed of wealth, comfort, and what we see today as the American dream (Luke 12:15–21). I told the story to my young friend, with a few details from my imagination thrown in.

A successful businessman entered his two-story, four-bedroom, new-build home in the Master Planned Community located a half-hour commute from downtown. He came from his windowed office on the fourteenth floor, a gift that accompanied his director-level position.

He strolled out to the back patio and sat down by the pool,

contemplating his good fortune in getting a raise that gave him access to a 30 percent bonus. He mused, "What will I do with this extra money? If I want to be smart, safe, and secure, and have plenty saved up for years to come, I'll spend my time buying more stocks that will make even more money. And I'll build a bigger house, with a four-car garage, so I can store my new truck and speedboat."

He leaned back with his arms behind his head, dreaming. "Then I can take life easy. I'll retire early, go on that cruise to Bali, and send my kids to any university they choose . . ."

Sounds nice, doesn't it? What might this look like in our own lives?

For our family, it seemed sensible and safe to stay in the United States, since we were in our forties, with children heading into high school. My husband and I owned a nice house in a lovely neighborhood and earned a comfortable income with medical insurance and a retirement plan.

But, let's remember that before telling the story of the businessman in Luke 12, Jesus said, "Beware! Guard against every kind of greed. Life is not measured by how much you own" (Luke 12:15). God called the businessman a fool and said, "This very night your life will be demanded of you. Then who will get what you have prepared for yourself?" Jesus went on to tell his disciples, "This is how it will be with whoever stores up things for themselves but is not rich toward God" (vv. 20–21 NIV).

We all die one day. It's just reality. I don't want to live my life just to pay the mortgage and go on a couple of vacations . . . and then die without an adventure with God. I want to live *rich toward God*. That means surrendering what most of the world tells us is important in life and doing what God tells us to do.

It's hard to imagine the American dream as anything but a worthy goal: wealth, financial security, comfort, and safety. We wish for a safe life with a steady income and a comfortable retirement. We hope to secure a good job, marry a good spouse, and buy a good house. If the American dream motivates most of our choices, moving overseas for the sake of the gospel *will* appear ludicrous.

In contrast, Jesus called us to lose our life in order to find it: "If any of you wants to be my follower, you must turn from your selfish ways, take up your cross, and follow me. If you try to hang on to your life, you will lose it. But if you give up your life for my sake, you will save it. And what do you benefit if you gain the whole world but lose your own soul? Is anything worth more than your soul?" (Matt. 16:24–26).

What do we need to give up in order to gain what God has for us? What do we need to relinquish in order to live rich toward God? We must surrender materialism. Surrender financial security. Surrender comfort. And surrender safety. After all, what is worth more than our souls?

Surrender Materialism

Materialism reigns as the unspoken and acceptable vice in Western cultures. It's a god we worship without calling it a god. We're motivated to buy more, buy bigger, buy better—to buy, buy, buy, and buy.

"It's not the money that's bad," said every preacher I've ever heard speaking on wealth or materialism. "What's bad is the hold that money can have on you." Even though this statement may ring true, it leaves a loophole. A single, guilt-free sentence assuring us that even though we all

> MATERIALISM REIGNS AS THE UNSPOKEN AND ACCEPTABLE VICE IN WESTERN CULTURES. IT'S A GOD WE WORSHIP WITHOUT CALLING IT A GOD.

have money, at least it *probably* doesn't have a hold on us. But who says it doesn't have a hold on us? It does on me! We may insist we don't struggle with materialism. If so, we may not be struggling with it. We may simply be yielding to its enticing temptation. Jesus doesn't pacify wealthy people. Instead, he says things like, "I'll say it again—it is easier for a camel to go through the eye of a needle than for a rich person to enter the Kingdom of God!" (Matt. 19:24).

I am that wealthy person living in one of the wealthiest countries in the world, and this terrifies me. It terrifies me that I might be the wealthy person who lives numb to the fact that I'm trying to squeeze myself through a hole in the needle. Until I surrender this area of my life to Jesus, he is the only one with the ability to make me small enough to fit through the eye of that needle.

When our family first contemplated moving to India, we knew it also meant selling most of our possessions. The process of determining what to keep and what to toss or sell was both sobering and freeing.

The first garage sale felt easy. We de-cluttered and sold outgrown children's clothes, extra sets of dishes, and old furniture I didn't like. But after that sale, our house still looked exactly the same. It didn't appear we'd sold much of anything.

We held a second garage sale, the kind that said, "Everything must go!" This one hurt more. I sensed an inward struggle. I priced a beloved dining room table with wrought-iron chair backs too high. No one thought it worth $300 at a garage sale, so no one bought it. I felt sick as people carted off our things, bargaining down to a dollar or two. I ran outside and grabbed that thingamajig out of a bargaining customer's hand before she acquired a $20 item for $1.

"I still need that!" I gasped. "I didn't mean to sell it quite yet!"

My husband finally shut down the garage sale early and said, "Get a grip. If you don't want to sell all of this for a few dollars, then don't sell it at all!"

My time to surrender materialism came at this moment. When we have to surrender something, it will be a struggle. It will be hard. If it doesn't involve a wrestling match with either God or our flesh, then I wouldn't call it surrender. Selling our torn-up couch set didn't feel like surrender. We had owned it for nineteen years, and it boasted rips and tears and sunken springs. I was happy to get rid of it.

But then I looked at my dining room table, along with the rest of the things I just couldn't quite give up. I asked God to reveal why surrendering that dining room table felt so hard. He spoke to my soul. "You don't trust that I can give you another table like that one ever again. The thing is, you don't need this table right now. Let it go, and trust that if and when you need another table, I'll make sure you get one. Even if you never get another table like this, can you live with that? Can you give it up to move to India for me?"

I crumbled and humbled. It felt like such a small thing. Who wouldn't be willing to give up a table to walk with Jesus on an adventure to a place where millions wait in a shadow of darkness without the light of Jesus? A table or people's souls? No question. I gave it up and decided to trust God.

God softened the grip of materialism on my soul, and later spoke to me from the Bible. In the story of the rich young ruler, Jesus said, "Sell all your possessions and give the money to the poor, and you will have treasure in heaven. Then come, follow me" (Luke 18:22).

Jesus didn't say, "Sell everything you have at garage sale prices to people who already have too much stuff, and try to get the best deal you can."

"Who are the poor around me, God?" I asked. Everyone I knew already had a dining room table. God brought to mind the new refugees coming into our city. I contacted the refugee resettlement agency and found out a Sudanese family with two young children would arrive that week, with only a few suitcases to their name.

After that initial surrender, in which I trusted Jesus to provide even a future dining table for our family, our family joyfully gave the rest of our things to this Sudanese family. Our nicest things that I didn't, or wouldn't, sell—furniture, rugs, drapes, and accessories—furnished an entire apartment. It felt right. It felt like obedience. It felt like losing our life to find it.

We then asked our children to choose what would fill their suitcases to bring to India. One suitcase each for clothes and one suitcase each for extras, like toys. When we stood at the airport, ready to board the plane for what we assumed would be decades away from America, all we owned filled the plastic tubs at our feet, plus some cash in the bank, along with our memories stashed away in the five-by-ten-foot storage unit.

I never felt freer financially.

I'm aware, though, that the lure of materialism lurks in the shadows, never far away. And so, every day we must relinquish materialism as our god. God is our God. Seize the day!

Let's pause for a moment to pray together to surrender materialism:

God, I hold out my hands to you with my palms up. Please show me what possession I love more than you, and let me visualize it in my hands. I confess that I love this thing more than I love you. How can I imagine letting you have it right now? Show me what you will do with this possession if I let you own it. My hands are still open, God. Show me what you will give me spiritually, in return for relinquishing the hold this possession has on my life.

Now hold out your hands again. Repeat this prayer until God shows you every possession that keeps you from a potential future that might require you to relinquish it.

Surrender Financial Security

Materialism, which beckons us to acquire possessions, is twin to another idol: financial security. We won't be free to follow God anywhere he asks us until we can place our financial security in the hands of a God who promises to provide for us as we follow Him.

My parents lived on half the income most field workers made the majority of their lives. They followed God on one spiritual adventure after another for fifty years, moving to the Philippines, then America, and then to India and back again. Their knees boast spiritual callouses from the many times they asked God to give them the faith and the finances to embark on ventures that others called foolhardy. They purposed to stay out of debt, saving when they could. As a personal conviction, mirroring Hudson Taylor's faith-based missions model, they didn't ask others for funding, but only asked God.

They also prayed often. Growing up, our family didn't have designer clothes, and we didn't take designer vacations. But we never went hungry. We never went into debt. In the paradox principle of gaining by losing, all three of us children attended an international school for expatriates and went to private universities debt-free. Before even graduating from high school, I had already visited all fifty states and five countries.

I remember my mother wondering, and sometimes worrying, about how God might provide for her and my father in their old age. Certainly, they couldn't depend on substantial retirement savings, and at that time they didn't own any property to sell.

But just before my parents both turned sixty-five, a rich uncle died. Relatives found massive amounts of cash in his bank account and stashed throughout his old farm homestead. He left a will that perhaps God ordained from the beginning, bequeathing a substantial amount to my parents.

"You followed me," I could hear Jesus saying gently to my parents. "You dropped your fishing nets, and you left your father and your mother. You followed me, not knowing where I would lead you or how I would provide for you. Now, here's the next installment of my paycheck for you. Not millions, but just enough to supplement your future here on earth."

Do you know what they did with that gift? They gave away a large percentage. They knew the acquisition of large amounts of money wasn't necessary for future financial security, so it seemed prudent to them to use the money for present needs and the advancement of the gospel. People who surrender financial security also tend to be generous givers.

To those waiting for retirement to "do something important for God," don't wait! Surrender the fear of losing financial security. Don't succumb to the worldly belief that it's foolish to give up a career or a pension or a retirement fund. The fact is, we may have money in the future, or we may not. We may have health then, or we may not. We may be close enough to hear God then, or we may not.

If you sense God nudging your heart toward making disciples in other cultures, don't miss your opportunity because you're holding so tightly to the world's idea of financial security. I've never heard anyone who chose the life of a long-term field worker say, "I wish I would have stayed in my career and worked sixty hours a week for an employer selling nuts and bolts instead of doing this." Never. I've never heard of any field workers say they wouldn't do it all again, no matter how hard it felt or the suffering they endured or the lack of worldly possessions they owned.

On the other hand, I've heard plenty of older people and middle-income couples with home mortgages and 2.5 children say, "I wish I would have gone when I was younger. Why didn't I go? I should have gone. Now it's too late." With doubt and regret, they wish they had trusted God more fully with their financial security. Don't wait! No matter how old or how young we are, it's not too late to trust God with our future and our finances and see what he might ask us to do next.

We will relinquish financial security as our god. God is our God. Seize the day!

Now let's pray to surrender financial security:

God, please show me any fear I have about financial security. What is false about this fear? What is true about this fear? If I give up my perceived financial security to obey you in a way you're leading me, how will you provide for me? How does your Word assure me that you will take care of me if I give up everything to follow you? Jesus, show me how to give this fear to you and watch you nail it to the cross. Is there anything you want me to do practically to take a step toward releasing financial security into your care?

Surrender Comfort

I love my pillow. I love to slide into the 600-thread-count sheets on our bed with a double-foam mattress. I love curling up on our cushioned couch on a rainy day and reading a good book, eating warm chocolate chip cookies fresh from the oven.

I don't like to be hot and sticky. I don't really like to sleep on hard beds, sit on hard furniture, or dodge uninvited insects in my home. When it comes to manual labor, I'm fairly soft and lazy. I love to be comfortable. I confess it. This proved the hardest surrender for me in agreeing to move overseas.

"Just bury it in the dirt," said a local woman in India when we asked what to do with a huge, broken piece of glass, right after we moved. There wasn't any other place to put it. People told us the same thing when we asked what to do with a spoiled chicken.

At first, I felt betrayed by our standard of living, as I hung up each piece of laundry to dry, timing the washer around the power outages, smashing cockroaches and sweeping away ant armies regularly. We lived in a house—in a city. Not in some remote village, but it sure felt like one. We had come to India as businesspeople! I hadn't expected to have to muster up the courage to jump into a cold shower every day. We had wrestled our four school-age children away from friends and everything familiar and walked away from well-paying jobs. I thought *that* was the hard part.

No. Cooking, cleaning, and living each day in India gave me new understanding of surrender and fortitude—not to mention good old-fashioned work.

I assembled breakfast, lunch, dinner, and snacks for four hungry American children and one very, very American husband by using curry, cumin, rice, eggs, and chicken—which I couldn't find without witnessing the slitting of a throat and carrying it home in a warm, bloody bag. No real cheese. No tortilla chips. No ranch dressing. No granola bars or Fruit Roll-Ups. No Costco or Wal-Mart. Grocery shopping involved a rickshaw ride from the teeming city or a long walk as I dragged only the bags I could carry in two hands. I chopped vegetables from the market after hours of soaking them in vinegar. All of this while sweating profusely 100 percent of the time, my hair slicked back in a permanently greased, flathead ponytail. I was *not* comfortable!

Fast-forward six months later and I found myself writing:

A bedtime routine I never dreamed I would have: draw two buckets of water from the well to heat up for hot bucket showers, hand-washing dishes, and filling the water purifier for drinking. Tie up the food waste plastic bag and trash to put outside for the morning trash ladies (at least we don't have to burn it anymore). Hang up the laundry on a clothesline for drying under the bedroom fans at night. Then I cuddle with the kids in bed, listening to the monsoon rain and the night jungle noises from our open windows, feeling quite pioneer-like and wholesome.

Yes, my routine did grow into something normal and natural. But it still required daily perseverance and a conscious choice to die to comfort. It took stamina and endurance to live overseas. But it turned out okay. I finally figured out where to bury the glass and the spoiled chicken.

We will surrender comfort as our god. God is our God. Seize the day!

Let's pray and ask God how we can surrender comfort:

God, please show me what I love about being comfortable. Please show me the very specific things I turn to for comfort that I'll need to give up if I follow you to a different country. I confess my selfishness and my self-centeredness. Help me to want to give up living an easy life. Please forgive me for letting the comforts of this earthly life keep me from considering any other way that you might ask me to live. Lord, if I give up this comfort, this ease of living, how will you help me to survive without it? How can I practice giving it up now, practicing perseverance in physical discomfort?

Surrender Safety

Terrorists. Typhoid. Typhoons. Just the thought of traveling in an airplane may give us pause. In the Western world, we wear seat belts. We lock our doors. We install security systems in our homes. Churches provide check-in procedures with matching tags for parents to safely pick up their children from Sunday school. Some fight for the right to bear arms, in the name of safety. Some fight for the right to eliminate arms, in the name of safety. We vaccinate—even our pets. Or we don't vaccinate, also in the name of safety.

I'm thankful for all the ways our country values keeping us safe. Safe from terrorists. Safe from needless death. Safe from war. The *pursuit of safety* is a high value for Westerners. But if our own safety is of higher value than obeying God, we won't consider a calling that involves the potential of danger. It's not natural to consider an option that demands running *into* the pain, *into* the fray, *into* danger instead of *away* from it. The high value of safety as a personal right can distract us from God's calling on our lives. Many of us have bought into the lie that God would never ask us to live somewhere where disease, danger, and maybe even death are real possibilities. But he might have different plans.

Could we choose to live in an apartment complex with international students next to a university instead of a master-planned suburb with good schools for our children? Or buy a house in a lower-class neighborhood where Sudanese refugees can afford housing instead of a property that would increase in value over time? How about moving to Cairo to run a language school instead of teaching high school in our hometown?

If you become a long-term field worker, it is most likely *not safer* where you will go in the future than where you are now. Few of the places where unreached people groups live are safer. Some, in fact, are quite dangerous. Grandparents, even godly ones, understandably feel concern for their grandchildren brought across the ocean to live with Muslims or Buddhists or Hindus. Even if you decide to move to inner-city New York, into a community of immigrants, some people will question your decision. Well-meaning Christians will sit you down and tell you that you are acting foolishly. Many will not understand.

How do we release our natural desire for safety to God, so that he can free us to chart the course of our lives in response to his leading? Let's ask God to help us believe these three truths as we develop a theology of safety.

Truth #1: God is our protection.

The physical view of safety—as something attainable, as something real—can cloud the spiritual view of safety. But the psalmist reminds us, "God is our refuge and strength, always ready to help in times of trouble" (Ps. 46:1). *God* is our refuge, not people, not places, not seat belts. We can live in the safest country in the world, with all the correct safety controls in place, and still get hit by another car on the freeway. Bad things can still happen, even in our hometowns.

Pursued by those who wish to kill him, King David wrote, "Some nations boast of their chariots and horses, but we boast in the name of the Lord our God" (Ps. 20:7).

When we move out of a place that feels safe, we learn to recognize that our true protection and our true safety is, and always has been, in the hands of God. In some countries, we can no longer trust in the seat belts, because there aren't any. We can no longer trust in orderly road behavior, because one lane becomes five and red lights are simply suggestions. We can't trust in the police to keep us safe, because the police can be bribed by money or power.

We learn to pray prayers of safety daily, sometimes hourly, as we're packed into a bus with a hundred other people (and chickens), lurching around hairpin turns up a mountain with

> WHEN WE MOVE OUT OF A PLACE THAT FEELS SAFE, WE LEARN TO RECOGNIZE THAT OUR TRUE PROTECTION AND OUR TRUE SAFETY IS, AND ALWAYS HAS BEEN, IN THE HANDS OF GOD.

cliffs on both sides. We recognize that God is our protection, both back home *and* in the rest of the world.

This frees us to say, "Yes, God, I will move somewhere that is less safe, because you are our protection."

Truth #2: God knows when and how we will die.

The way we view the sovereignty of God informs our decisions when he asks us to move to risky places. As Job said when confronted with great loss and an uncertain future, "You have decided the length of our lives. You know how many months we will live, and we are not given a minute longer" (Job 14:5). If we believe that God plans out our days and knows when we will leave this earth (Ps. 139:16), we can go anywhere he leads us without fear.

In war, the cost of freedom isn't cheap. Freedom is bought with flesh and blood, the lives of our own brothers and sisters. Even in spiritual war, freedom isn't cheap. Throughout history, Christians have paid a great price to enter new territory with the gospel. There are no guarantees.

Tears always come when I remember the cost that faithful field workers paid in their adopted countries. Hudson Taylor buried his daughter and his beloved wife in China. Elisabeth Elliot and four other women buried their husbands in the jungles of South America. Martin and Gracia Burnham spent a year kidnapped by al-Qaeda in the Philippines before Martin entered heaven as a martyr. In more recent times, a terrorist entered the home of a Western doctor in Afghanistan and shot and killed her husband and two teenage children.

These followers of Christ are now clothed in white robes before the throne, shouting, "O Sovereign Lord, holy and true, how long before you judge the people who belong to this world and avenge our blood for what they have done to us?" (Rev. 6:10).

We must trust God with the number of our days. If the number of my days is short, then I want each day to count.

Truth #3: Jesus will be with us.

When Jesus told his disciples to go into all the world, he ended with a promise: "And be sure of this: I am with you always, even to the end of the age" (Matt. 28:20). The truth of Jesus' presence gives us courage, confidence, and comfort in our calling.

Jesus is *present* in every situation and in every place. As believers, we are filled with the Spirit of Christ. He goes with us wherever we go (Gal. 2:20). We can speak to him when we're afraid, and he can speak to us. When we wrestle with God about vital matters of safety, the Holy Spirit can tell us what we need to know to persevere or change course (John 16:13–15).

Every morning while living in Iraq, field workers James and Donnah, the ones who led Yusef in chapter 5 to the Lord, put their middle school children in a car with a hired driver and watched them drive away, weaving through the Green Zone on their way to school. Every day, they prayed until they received the phone call telling them the car made it safely to school. Every day, they heard bombs going off around them in the distant city. At a breaking point of stress, James went up to their flat rooftop overlooking the city.

He cried out to God, "I'm afraid. I'm too afraid. I need to know if we should go home or stay. I need to know if my children are going to be safe. If I need to surrender them, I need to know this. But if they are going to be safe, I want to be free from this worry."

He looked to the north on his rooftop landing. A large man in full US Army gear with machine guns stood at the edge of the roof, watching to the north. James looked to the opposite corner of the rooftop and saw another man, in the same gear, watching over the south. Four men stood guarding the place. No United States soldiers remained in the city at that time. They were not soldiers.

God opened James's eyes to the realities of the heavenly world in that moment. God assured him that he wanted them to stay in this city, in that time, and in that place until he instructed them to move. They ran to the pain, bringing Christ's freedom to a place that did not feel free or safe.

We will relinquish safety as our god! God is our God. Seize the day!

Let's pray together to surrender our safety:

I confess I believe the lie that my own devices are really what protect me—and that I can control the number of my days. Help me to believe the truth that you have chosen the number of my days. I choose to spend those days in pursuit of you and not let fear keep me from fulfilling the purposes you have for me. I now name everyone for whose safety I fear—because I'm bringing them with me, or leaving them behind. What do you want me to know about them? Show me how I can give you this fear and be free from it. In the name of Jesus Christ, will you open my eyes to the heavenly world and the forces of protection that you have assigned to those who love you? (Ps. 91:11). Thank you.

Reflection

1. What parts of the American dream—wealth, financial security, comfort, and safety—did you grow up believing were important to pursue and achieve?

2. Which of the prayers of surrender seemed hardest for you to pray: surrendering wealth, financial security, comfort, or safety? Why?

3. Ask God to give you ideas on how you can tangibly practice surrendering something in each category, little by little, even in the next week.

TWELVE

Getting Healthy and Hearing from God

"God, how can I keep my kindness?" I prayed through the *swish, swish* of my rattan swing. "I don't think people yell at each other in heaven," I mused.

Our move to hot and humid India catapulted me into physical, spiritual, and emotional stress I hadn't experienced before. The fuse on my emotional firecracker, usually plenty long and snuffed out before it reached its destination, lay one inch to detonation.

In the evening, I rocked in the rattan swing—a cradle chair hanging by a chain from the ceiling—to unwind and *swish* away the stress. Sinking into the rounded seat, the edges wrapped around me, hiding me from the stifling heat, the damp musty air, and the cockroaches scuttling on the floor. The tiredness of a day filled with an unfamiliar brand of physical labor and constant people fell into that swing.

Tending to the fruit of the Spirit took more patience and practice in that place than in my suburban American home. There, kind words came easily with the comfort of full-time electricity, an inside temperature set at an unchanging 78 degrees Fahrenheit, a car I could drive at any time of day or night, with grocery stores minutes away. I could refuel spiritually just around the corner at a church with energetic, quality worship.

When we first arrived in India, we all felt hungry from eating unfamiliar foods. We felt deprived of luxuries such as packaged cereal, deli lunch meat, and spaghetti sauce in a jar. We slept on thin floor mattresses, all six of us in the one room that had a semi-functioning air conditioner, robbing us of sleep. We couldn't understand local people. Everyone stared at us. Times with God withered in the midst of an ever-changing schedule. The electricity shut off randomly—as did the water. And the heat, with inside temperatures of 90 degrees and 90 percent humidity, pressed in on us like steam inside a pressure cooker.

We lived with the pressurized steam constant and whistling, stifled under a thin layer of forced civility, ready to blow at any moment. We operated on the bottom rung of Maslow's hierarchy—where survival is all we could focus on and the top rung of self-awareness disappeared. And when someone lives on the bottom rung, desperate for physical survival, the ability to use nice words disappears. There at the bottom, the margin to be kind disappeared.

So my husband and I sat all four children down around the table one day and said, "We acknowledge our weakness. Only a paper-thin cushion separates the way we feel from us *acting* on the way we feel. So, today, our goal is kindness. That's it. We'll speak in kindness to each other. We'll act in kind ways to each other. That's the goal for today."

With these words, we entered a season of abandoning our familiar ways of coping. We practiced perseverance and curbed our selfishness. We sharpened our ability to suffer in silence and cooled the fires of anger that easily erupted so that peace could enter our home once again.

We imagined how our ugly words—the spewing of our discomfort and our disappointment—turned to black oil all over the other person. We pictured ourselves donning ethereal gowns called kindness, and we relished their imaginary cooling effects. To be kind meant keeping that sticky awfulness to ourselves and exchanging it for cooling robes of grace.

Over time, I found myself able to endure more heat and more stickiness. I kept silent more often and dismissed the gnawing wish for an ice-cold Diet Pepsi. We played worship music in our home and guarded our personal times with God.

After winning a few of the day's battles to persevere in kindness, India would blow an evening breeze of peace. And I would *swish, swish* into a quiet rest and hear the sounds of the city: a barking dog, the neighbor *pat-patting* chapatis on a flat stone, crickets chirping, even the added swishes of a hundred bats stirring from their upside-down slumbers on the banana trees next to our veranda.

Clothed in kindness, little by little, we stopped yelling on earth, as it is in heaven.

What's Inside *Will* Come Out

When we move overseas, the insides of our souls land on the other side of the world like a beached whale, in plain view for all to see. We squirm to wiggle back into the familiar ocean of normalcy to hide our insecurity, our unhealed wounds, or our character deficiencies. But no. They will sit out there in plain view, a spectacle, until we deal with them.

Whatever is lurking in the dark corners of our souls—our weaknesses, our struggles, our secret sins—*will* come out for

> WHATEVER IS LURKING IN THE DARK CORNERS OF OUR SOULS—OUR WEAKNESSES, OUR STRUGGLES, OUR SECRET SINS—*WILL* COME OUT FOR EVERYONE TO SEE.

everyone to see. It will unearth the cracks in our character, the rough edges of our personality, and the trauma that never healed.

While we'll never be perfect—or perfectly ready—to go, we can pursue spiritual and emotional wholeness ahead of time. This will decrease the dredge of spiritual and emotional messiness that surfaces in us when we land. Knowing how to process through the following five steps with God in a place that is familiar to us, with people who know us, will equip us to do it well when everything and everyone around us is foreign.

#1: Embrace your identity in Christ.

It's important to know who you are, and whose you are.

In the Bible, Jeshua, a would-be high priest chosen for a special purpose, didn't feel special or purposeful. In a vision, Jeshua is transported to heaven for a moment, but he's dressed in filthy clothing. Poor Jeshua, his head down, eyes lowered, cowered before the courts of heaven as "the Accuser, Satan, was there at the angel's right hand, making accusations against Jeshua. And the LORD said to Satan, 'I the LORD, reject your accusations, Satan'" (Zech. 3:1–2).

The Lord *rejected* Satan's accusations. An angel instructed others standing there to take Jeshua's filthy clothes and dress him in clean ones. He spoke directly to Jeshua, "See, I have taken away your sins, and now I am giving you these fine new clothes" (v. 4).

Imagine Jeshua walking around in his fine new clothes. But if he still *feels* like he's wearing his filthy, dirty clothes, he will certainly not act like a chosen emissary of the King. He needs to embrace the new identity that comes with his new clothes.

You, too, are dressed in fine, new clothes. You are dressed in the righteousness of Christ, adopted into God's family, heirs to eternity (Rom. 8:14–17). Have you embraced the truths about yourself that come with these fine, new clothes?

Alicia didn't feel beautiful, even though God had clothed her in the righteousness of Christ. She didn't feel smart. She didn't feel loved. But she never told anyone this. She repeated what she heard from other Christians: "I know that Jesus covers my sin and when God looks at me, he sees Jesus." But did he see *her*? she wondered. As she prepared to move overseas, Kathryn, a field preparation coach at her sending agency, observed her insecurities. One day Kathryn asked Alicia if she wanted freedom in that area.

Earlier that morning, Alicia had read the verse, "For we are God's masterpiece. He has created us anew in Christ Jesus, so we can do the good things he planned for us long ago" (Eph. 2:10). As she and her coach prayed, she saw herself as that masterpiece, wearing a beautiful gown and holding a scepter that had power in the spiritual world. When her coach prayed that same verse over her without knowing its significance, Alicia knew God wanted to break through to her heart. With tears, she heard Jesus speaking to her, deep in her being, "You are a daughter of the King. I love you and I made you. I think you're lovely."

Alicia moved overseas, confident of her identity in Christ. She now uses her spiritual scepter, praying with other women also struggling with their identities. She can do this, because she knows who she is and whose she is.

Let's pray this prayer to affirm our identities in Christ:

Jesus, how do you view me? Please show me what it looks like to be dressed in the righteousness of Christ. What is the enemy still accusing me of in regard to my identity in you? What is the truth about that accusation, God? What is your name for me? Thank you for how you've chosen me for a purpose. Help me to walk in confidence, knowing I belong to you.

#2: Believe the truth about who God is.

What we believe about God—what we *really* believe—will shape our actions, conversations, and aspirations. Satan tries to destroy us by planting lies in our minds about God, even in our childhood. "It wasn't growing up in less than ideal circumstances that placed me in bondage," wrote Rusty Rustenbach in *A Guide for Listening and Inner-Healing Prayer*. "The problem was the lie I believed and the faulty strategies that evolved as a result."[1]

Jesus said of Satan, "He was a murderer from the beginning. He has always hated the truth, because there is no truth in him. When he lies, it is consistent with his character; for he is a liar and the father of lies" (John 8:44).

Even in the garden of Eden, Satan used the strategy of deception to undermine God. He sidled up to Eve and suggested slyly, "Did God *really* say you must not eat the fruit from any of the trees in the garden?" (Gen. 3:1, emphasis added). He sowed the seed of doubt about what God said to her, twisting God's words.

Lies we believe about God limit our trust in his ability to act. The road to the field requires perseverance and suffering, and we'll need to know that we know the truths of God's promises. We'll need to believe he is who he says he is—and that he intends good for us. When sickness, death, disappointment, discouragement, depression, or something else overwhelms us in a sea of doubt, we still won't quit.

After three months in his new country, Joe lost sixty pounds from a stomach illness—the kind that Westerners in developing countries fear. He fell far behind his peers in language classes. Dark images in nightmares started to plague his nights.

He read, "Taste and see that the LORD is good. Oh, the joys of those who take refuge in him!" (Ps. 34:8). But Joe didn't taste anything good, and he didn't feel any joy. Sick, disillusioned, and disturbed, he began to doubt the character of God.

In his journal, Joe admitted, "God, I don't trust you. I don't trust that you can help me, or that you even want to help me, or that you are good to me. You didn't heal me. You didn't touch my mouth and make language come easily for me. Now you're letting the devil torture me in my sleep. You let me down, and I don't trust you." What he read about God in scripture was just the opposite, but it was difficult to receive the truth in his soul because of his overwhelming circumstances. He had come with an inexperienced and deficient view of God, and he returned home a broken man.

When God's people doubt his love and his intent for goodness in their lives, Satan gains a foothold. He knows he has an opportunity to steal the rich and satisfying life God intended for us to live. Jesus said, "The thief's purpose is to steal and kill and destroy. My purpose is to give them a rich and satisfying life" (John 10:10).

When Joe returned home, he wrestled with his disappointment but stopped praying and reading scripture. He tried to surrender his disappointment about God's goodness, and in the process he experienced aspects of the Lord in personal, practical ways. He experienced Yahweh-Yireh, which means "the LORD will provide" (Gen. 22:14), when God graciously returned his previous career to him. He experienced El HaNe'eman, which means "the faithful God" (Deut. 7:9), when a friend prayed with him for new perspective on his situation overseas. He saw that God did heal his body, even though it took longer than he wanted. And God hadn't promised to make language easy, but only to put words in his mouth when he needed it. He experienced Jehovah Rapha, "the Lord who heals" (Ex. 15:26), when angels fought the darkness in his nightmares. When a friend prayed in the name of Jesus Christ for the dreams to leave him, they stopped.

You, too, can strengthen your trust in God's character. Choose one of the names of God in the Bible. You can find a few at https://bible. org/article/names-god. Ask yourself if you truly believe that aspect of

God in your life. Remember when you previously experienced God in that way. Do a Bible study on the promises of God. Declare every promise out loud. For example, "Lord, I receive the truth that you will personally go ahead of me. You will neither fail me nor abandon me" (Deut. 31:6).

"There is a world of difference between knowing something to be true in your head and experiencing the reality in your life," wrote Henry and Richard Blackaby and Claude King in *Experiencing God: Knowing and Doing the Will of God.*[2]

Ask the Lord to reveal truth to you about any aspect of his nature that you doubt. Spend time in gratitude, thanksgiving, and praise in the spirit of Psalm 34:3: "Come, let us tell of the LORD's greatness; let us exalt his name together."

Let's pray this prayer to ask God to help us believe all of who he says he is:

God, I want to know you in a personal way. Please don't let Satan deceive me by causing me to doubt your promises, your character, or your goodness. I want to believe that you are who you say you are and that you will do what you say you will do. Show me how I have experienced you as good, powerful, present, and active in my life.

#3: Receive healing from inner wounds or trauma.

Many people walk around with an invisible emotional limp. The limp is usually an unhealed heart wound from a loss, trauma, or sin. It's hard to care about the nations—or other people—if we're bleeding on the inside from our own wounds. We can't offer healing to others— especially in an unfamiliar culture with an unfamiliar people—if we're not healed ourselves. We can't give away what we don't have.

I learned this during a time of brokenness in my own life. In a desperate season when my competence, education, and knowledge failed me, I experienced a deep disappointment and prolonged discouragement I could not overcome. After several traumatic, sudden losses, I saw myself on an operating table, my heart cut open and bleeding out everywhere. I needed a surgeon. But I didn't know any surgeons who could sew up an invisible heart wound. I felt helpless in my brokenness, both by wounds inflicted by my own poor decisions and hurts I felt from others.

Another woman, plagued with literal bleeding for twelve years, couldn't find any surgeons for her wounds, either. When she noticed Jesus passing by in a crowd, she knew that if she could just get to him—if she could just touch the edge of his cloak—he could stop her bleeding.

I searched desperately, like this woman, for any medicine or doctor that might heal me. I longed for God to be present in my current circumstances, and I begged, "Must I wait until heaven for everything to be made right? I need someone to show up and rescue me from myself and from a life you didn't mean for me to live. I need it to matter right now, right here."

One day, I realized that unless I could touch Jesus, I would bleed to death on this emotional operating table. I found a friend who knew how to help broken people touch Jesus through inner healing prayer. Jesus, who heals people by the authority of God. Jesus, who breathes peace into people's souls. Jesus, who speaks truth against the lies of the enemy. I reached out to grab onto the edge of his cloak. If I could just reach the edge of his sleeve. . . .

When I cried myself to sleep as an adult in desperate need of saving on earth, even though I was already saved for heaven, God listened. The invisible, strong hand of Jesus pressed a compress to my heart to stop the bleeding. In Scripture, Jesus instantly stopped the woman's bleeding too. For twelve years she had carried this pain, and he stopped it instantly. When she touched the hem of his robe in a crowd, Jesus asked who had touched him because he felt power go out from him. By revealing her identity and her need, she gave him her faith, without conditions and without knowing exactly what would happen or what he would say. In return, Jesus Christ gave her more than physical healing. He gave her peace: "Daughter," he said, "your faith has made you well. Go in peace. Your suffering is over" (Mark 5:34). Although scars still remain, over time, Jesus sewed up my broken heart. My husband and I listened with courage and wisdom to Jesus guiding our family. He lifted my deep discouragement by leading us in a new direction—and replaced my desperate disappointment with new dreams.

Now I can freely give away what I've received—hope, healing, emotional health, Jesus. Before you set foot on foreign soil, before you even go to sleep tonight—let Jesus bring healing to your heart.

Pray this prayer for courage to seek healing:

Jesus, I don't want to walk around wounded anymore. Please free me from this pain inside of me. Show me how to let it go and give it to you so that I can receive your joy, peace, and hope. Please stop the bleeding in my heart. Give me courage to seek prayer and counseling so I can deal with painful things in my past. Thank you for loving me enough to want me to be free.

#4: Deal with sin.

"Where sin is, God is not," said a wise ninety-two-year-old who lived as a field worker in Africa most of his life. He knows that unconfessed, ongoing sin from an unrepentant heart blocks our relationship with the Lord God. The Old Testament is full of examples in which God stops responding when his people continue worshiping idols and refuse to repent. The prophet Isaiah warned an unrepentant Israel, "It's your sins that have cut you off from God. Because of your sins, he has turned away and will not listen anymore" (Isa. 59:2).

Even after we've received forgiveness from God, sin can rear its ugly head again, and its consequences can keep us entangled in its clutches if we don't deal with its root causes.

Nate struggled with pornography throughout his teenage years. One time, his parents found images on his phone and tried to help him, but his fascination with pornography continued. During a summer camp his senior year, he surrendered his life to Jesus and laid his pornography addiction on the altar of God's mercy and received forgiveness. With a repentant and resolved heart, he installed accountability software on all his electronic devices and asked his father to keep him accountable. By God's grace, he stopped viewing images and videos. But they still played in his mind. The temptation to relish those images often surfaced during times of stress.

Nate grew spiritually as he discipled nonbelievers on his secular university campus. His roommate, a student from the Middle East, gave his life to Jesus Christ. The experience launched Nate into friendships with other students from other countries. He found himself drawn to the nations, and, five years later, he and his new wife applied to move overseas with a sending agency. He wondered if they would consider him because of his past addiction and continuing temptation with pornography.

His field preparation coach challenged him to get full freedom from his addiction, something Nate didn't think possible. His coach spent hours in deep, healing prayer with Nate, and together they identified the lies the enemy had planted in Nate's mind about love, sex, and his own worth. Through the Holy Spirit during prayer, God revealed his truth to Nate about these things and confirmed it through the Word. Nate received a supernatural transformation and renewing of his mind, because he received God's truth about his own worth deep in his psyche, and it changed everything.

He and his wife also spent a year in marriage counseling, learning practical ways to communicate with each other and handle conflict in healthy ways, and they learned how to turn to God and each other in times of stress. Nate has now worked for more than thirty years in a fruitful, international role. He says that freedom from sinful practices and from memories of past sins is possible—and absolutely necessary.

Living overseas is stressful, and Nate still senses when the enemy tries to tempt him in this area. But he says now it feels as if Satan is just lobbing little spitballs through a straw at his mind. It bounces off a closed door instead of propelling through an open window and landing on its target. He is emotionally free, available to his wife, and effective in the kingdom of God.

Satan looks for weaknesses and previous sins to shame us and make us feel unworthy. He uses the lies we believe about ourselves or about God, and he exploits them. On the field, he will try the same lies and the same methods to destroy us as he did when we lived in our home country. So the first step is to lay down those weaknesses and confess our sins.

ON THE FIELD, SATAN WILL TRY THE SAME LIES AND THE SAME METHODS TO DESTROY US AS HE DID WHEN WE LIVED IN OUR HOME COUNTRY.

To "confess" means to "uncover" (see Job 31:33–34; Psalm 32). If we uncover our sins and find Jesus covering us by his blood, then Satan is handicapped. He no longer has a secret he can hold against us. If anything comes to mind at this moment, uncover your sin in all its ugliness and shame, and let Jesus cover you. If you uncover it now, it won't surface later when you least expect it.

God says, "I—yes, I alone—will blot out your sins for my own sake and will never think of them again" (Isa. 43:25). Before you go overseas, get freedom from addiction, from past sins, and from lies that keep you trapped. Then you can go and be whole—and wholly available—to those you're sent to serve.

We can all pray this prayer to lay down any secret sins:

God, you know my heart. You know where my flesh is weak. You know where I struggle and where I fail. Please forgive me for how I've dishonored your name by my sinful actions and thoughts. Bring what lurks in darkness into the light. Take this sin from me and nail it to the cross. Give me victory in this area, by the power of Jesus' name.

#5: Forgive others.

Unforgiveness carves deep gashes into our souls. It destroys our relationships with others and distorts our view of God. It comes like a gnawing ache, an ever-present pit in the stomach, a tumor that grows and crowds out joy. Sometimes unforgiveness gets stuffed down deep. It can even manifest as lower back pain, migraines, inflammation, or some other sickness in our physical bodies. Unforgiveness is easy to dismiss as small and insignificant, so it's easy to bring overseas, not realizing the damage it can cause in our hearts and our relationships with others.

God takes forgiveness seriously. Jesus said, "But if you refuse to forgive others, your Father will not forgive your sins" (Matt. 6:15). If we bring unforgiveness overseas with us, it won't go away just because we are working full-time for God. It will fester, harden, and the seed of bitterness will grow roots. It will crowd out our closeness to Jesus. We need this closeness to handle the suffering and stress required to live in difficult places.

I've seen unforgiveness cripple me. As we prepared to move overseas, I struggled to quench a growing bitterness in my heart from a long-past hurt that kept surfacing. My husband, watching me drown in my pitiful refusal to forgive, urged me to spend time in my prayer closet. "Don't come out until you do some business with God," he suggested. To the kids he said, "Don't bother Mommy. She might be in there awhile."

Sitting on the carpet in the dark, surrounded by clothes and musty shoes, I pled with God. I told him I didn't feel like forgiving. I didn't want to forgive. The person didn't deserve to be forgiven. I wanted to hold that unforgiveness and stroke it and feel sorry for myself.

God brought to mind the verse, "If you openly declare that Jesus is Lord and believe in your heart that God raised him from the dead, you will be saved" (Rom. 10:9). In context, the verse is about speaking out loud a truth about God and receiving salvation. But in my closet, I wondered if "openly declaring" my forgiveness could also "save" me from this obsession consuming me.

There's power in saying words out loud, even if we don't yet believe the words. So I talked to God, out loud, in the closet. "I forgive this person for this exact thing, and that thing, and this other thing—even though they won't talk about it, and even though they don't admit they did anything wrong to me. God, it hurts how they treated me. Please help me forgive this person." A flood of tears followed. Gutwrenching. Honest. I felt purged afterwards. Purged and clean. A weight, a burden, and hurt lifted off of me like ugly, black tar peeling off the skin of my soul. Relief. Lightness. Light. Peace.

Later, when reminders of the offenses tried to creep back into my heart, they threatened to entangle me with their ugly vines. When Jesus said to forgive seventy times seven times, it might mean offering forgiveness toward the same person, even if he or she never repeats the offense, up to 490 times (Matt. 18:22)! So over the next few weeks, I said it out loud, wherever I happened to be, and stopped the seed of bitterness from growing. It didn't quite take 490 trips to the closet, but by the time we moved to India, God had freed me from that person's power over me because of my unforgiveness. I could freely and wholly invest in new relationships without the shadow of former ones haunting me.

Are you burying or feeding any unforgiveness? Are you holding on to it, lugging it around like a backpack of rocks? Let's pray this prayer to start to let go of that burden:

> *Lord God, show me the name of anyone I refuse to forgive. By your power, give me strength to forgive _____ for what [he or she] did to me. I will say that person's name out loud, God, and name the offenses I harbor against [him or her]. I forgive each person for each offense by the blood of the Lord Jesus Christ and the power of the Holy Spirit in me. I free myself from carrying around this bitterness, and I bless them.*

Hearing from God

The Spirit of Christ lives inside of us. He speaks. He guides, convicts, encourages, and comforts (John 14:26; 16:8; Acts 9:31; Rom. 8:26). He can guide, convict, encourage, and comfort us through all five of the crucial steps we just discussed: embracing our identity, understanding God's identity, receiving healing of inner woundedness, dealing with sin, and purging unforgiveness. And when we land on foreign soil, we'll be glad we learned to hear his voice.

Jesus said, "My sheep listen to my voice. I know them and they follow me" (John 10:27). Sheep can discern the voice of their master from other voices. They listen to and obey the voice they know and trust. God speaks through scripture, through other people, and through circumstances (Jonah 1–4; 1 Cor. 14:3; 2 Tim. 3:16). He speaks through dreams, visions, and stories (Genesis 37, Matt. 13:3; Rev. 1:11). In the past, he's even spoken through a cloud, a burning bush, and through angels with a message (Ex. 3:2–14; 24:16; Luke 1:26–38).

If we quiet ourselves to listen, God also speaks directly to us through the Holy Spirit in us (Mark 13:11; John 16:13; Acts 8:29, 1 Cor. 2:13). As we read scripture, as we talk with other godly people, as we live our lives, we can ask the Holy Spirit to interpret and share God's mind and heart with us on a matter. But remember that God is not a Magic 8-Ball that we shake to get an answer and then put back on the shelf. He is relational and wants to speak to us in the context of relationship.

How do we hear the voice of the Spirit, know that it is him, and obey it? With an open Bible and an open heart, we spend time listening to the Holy Spirit instead of doing all the talking in prayer. Søren Kierkegaard once observed, "A man prayed, and at first he thought that prayer was talking. But he became more and more quiet until in the end he realized that prayer is listening."[3]

Since some of us might only have experience with prayer as a one-way event from ourselves to God, here is advice on how to listen when we pray:

#1: Go to a quiet place.

To discern the still, small voice of the Holy Spirit clearly and consistently, it's helpful to place yourself in a quiet place with no interruptions (1 Kings 19:12–13). Quiet your mind by listening to worship music, sitting in silence, or reading scripture. Turn off your cell phone, and close your laptop. Keep a piece of paper to write down stray thoughts, such as grocery lists or to-dos for later. Spend time inviting the Holy Spirit to speak to you. With practice, you will soon be able to distinguish his commentary.

#2: Don't worry about whether you're hearing your own thoughts or God's thoughts.

The Spirit of God often communicates through our own thoughts, since he lives inside of us. Instead of getting stuck trying to separate your thoughts from God's thoughts, ask, "Is what I'm thinking consistent with scripture? Does this thought come with love and encouragement, or condemnation?"

If your thoughts or impressions are contrary to God's Word—or either accusatory and condemning—then you can safely discard those thoughts. Tell the enemy to go away in the name of Jesus Christ, and ask the Spirit of God to guide your thoughts instead (2 Cor. 10:5). The apostle John wrote, "But you belong to God, my dear children. You have already won a victory over those people, because the Spirit who lives in you is greater than the spirit who lives in the world" (1 John 4:4).

#3: Ask open-ended questions.

Keep questions open-ended instead of giving God only the two options of a yes or a no. In the Gospels, Jesus rarely answered a direct question with a simple yes or no. When you have to make a decision or resolve an unsettling feeling or conflict, ask an open-ended question: "Holy Spirit, what do you want me to know about this?"

For example, if God burdens you for a particular people group, don't ask, "Do you want me to go to the Pashtun of Pakistan?" but instead, "What do you want me to know about reaching the Pashtun of Pakistan?"

Wait. Listen. Write down everything you sense God saying. Don't analyze it. Keep asking more questions about what you sense to dig deeper. Keep writing it down. Then ask God to confirm it with scripture.

For example, when you ask the question about your role reaching the Pashtuns, if you hear the words in your mind, *"You're a champion of causes,"* write it down. Then ask more about that: "How do you want me to champion this cause?"

#4: Be patient.

Be willing to wait. You may sense a confirmation from God about something, but he may not reveal the timing or the plan of how it might come to pass. Abraham and Sarah waited years, well past their childbearing ages, before they saw the son God promised them (Gen.17:18).

A burden that perseveres over time is a good indication of its validity. Abuses in listening to God can happen especially in decisional prayers. When we want confirmation about a vocational, locational, or family decision—a job, a house, or a spouse—it's tempting to be impatient. If we act rashly in these areas without continual confirmation from God, scripture, and others, we may be moving ahead of God.

#5: Understand that God is just as concerned with our hearts as with our circumstances.

God often speaks in principles rather than with directives. When Paul the apostle asked for God to remove his thorn in the flesh, each time the Lord answered, "My grace is all you need. My power works best in weakness" (2 Cor. 12:9). This gave Paul strength to walk through the suffering. God didn't let him know if the burden would be taken away, and it wasn't. But God did use it to shape Paul's heart to become more like his.

In the Gospels, Jesus drilled down to the heart of the matter by asking questions. To the sick man he asked, "Would you like to get well?" (John 5:6). Then he healed him. Jesus asked Peter three times, "Simon son of John, do you love me?" (John 21:15–17). Then he gave

Peter the charge to shepherd the church. Jesus is still the same Jesus. Don't be surprised if he replies to your questions by asking *you* a question designed to drill down to the heart of the matter.

In response to the example question about the Pashtuns of Pakistan, he might ask you things like, "How much of your life are you willing to give up? Do you trust me with your children—or a future spouse?"

#6: Realize that it's possible there's a reason for the silence.

When we encounter a black wall of silence, we can check a few things that might be blocking our communication with God. Ask yourself:

"Do I have an unconfessed sin?" If so, confess it. Ask forgiveness from anyone you hurt and make it right.

"Is there anyone I have not forgiven?" If so, go to the person and forgive. If that's not possible, forgive the person by speaking it out loud to God.

"Is it because I'm not hearing what I expect to hear?" If so, ask more clarifying questions about what you're sensing from God. Maybe he already answered your prayer, but you didn't notice because it's not what you expected or wanted.

A Final Word

Putting everything into practice in this book will bring us closer to God's heart for the nations. But it doesn't guarantee that we will bear spiritual fruit. The fruit of the Spirit is love, joy, peace, kindness, patience, goodness, faithfulness, gentleness, and self-control (Gal. 5:22–23). And the fruit of sharing the gospel is many coming into the kingdom of God (Matt. 13:23). But one thing does guarantee spiritual fruit as we interact with the nations, and that is remaining—abiding—in Jesus Christ.

Jesus says, "Remain in me, and I will remain in you. For a branch cannot produce fruit if it is severed from the vine, and you cannot be fruitful unless you remain in me. Yes, I am the vine; you are the branches. Those who remain in me, and I in them, will produce much fruit. For apart from me you can do nothing" (John 15:5).

ONE THING DOES GUARANTEE SPIRITUAL FRUIT AS WE INTERACT WITH THE NATIONS, AND THAT IS REMAINING—ABIDING—IN JESUS CHRIST.

To "remain" means to stay, to wait, or to abide. Originally an active verb, it implies constant action, meaning to persistently and continuously stay. The branches stay connected to the vine, persistently and continuously absorbing nourishment from the source. If we walk closely with Jesus, letting him guide, inspire, comfort, and convict us, spiritual fruit will grow. *Much fruit.*

Hudson Taylor revealed abiding as the spiritual secret of his success in China when he wrote:

> Take time. Give God time to reveal Himself to you. Give yourself time to be silent and quiet before Him, waiting to receive, through the Spirit, the assurance of His presence with you, His power working in you. Take time to read His Word as in His presence, that from it you may know what He asks of you and what He promises you. Let the Word create around you, create within you a holy atmosphere, a holy heavenly light, in which your soul will be refreshed and strengthened for the work of daily life.[4]

Every veteran fruitful field worker I know would echo his words. Abide in Jesus. Whether you choose to stay or to go, remain in Jesus. You will bear fruit.

Are You Made to Go to the Nations?

For your learning benefit, take the FREE ten-minute

Made to Go Test at

www.madetogotest.com

[[logo to come]]

See how well you're doing practicing God's heart for the nations.

Find out where you land on the Made to Go scale and get customized next steps.

How to Use *Across the Street and Around the World*

For Individuals:

- Gather a few friends together to read one chapter at a time, practicing it and discussing it together. Use the Small Group Plan for the group format and the Small Group Bible Reading List for the scripture to study each week.
- Read the book. Take the free online Made to Go Test at www.madetogotest.com and review your results. Notice the chapters where you scored lower points. Read the chapter that corresponds to the lower points again and start practicing one or two suggestions from it. When you've practiced for a season and seen success, choose another chapter with lower scores to practice. Take the Made to Go Test again and notice where you've grown in practicing God's heart for the nations.

For Churches:

You can encourage the congregation to read the book during a month-long emphasis on reaching out both locally and globally. Much of the advice about following Jesus to the nations applies to reaching out to anyone who does not know Jesus Christ personally, as well as encouraging spiritual growth and health in all areas of life.

Follow or adapt the message plan below for a sermon series "Across the Street and Around the World":

Week One: Adopting God's Heart for the World (chapter 1)

POINT ONE: God blessed us to be a blessing to the nations (Gen. 12:1–3) (pp. **XX**).

POINT TWO: God confirms it through the Old Testament (Daniel, Esther, Jonah) (pp. **XX**).

POINT THREE: God confirms it in the New Testament—the disciples follow Jesus to the nations (pp. **XX**).

POINT FOUR: God planned for all nations to worship him (Rev. 5:1–10).

- Application for congregation: Eat this week at an ethnic restaurant.
- Interactive Idea: Ask the congregation to set their cell phone alarms for 5:09 p.m. to pray Revelation 5:9 each day for the nations that week.

Week Two: Making Disciples of the Nations Across the Street (chapters 2–4)

POINT ONE: Lay down our preferences for someone else (1 Cor. 9:19–29) (pp. **XX**).

POINT TWO: Welcome the foreigner—international students and refugees (Matt. 25:31–46 (pp. **XX**).

POINT THREE: Make disciples who make disciples (1 Tim. 2:2) (pp. **XX**).

- Application for congregation: Ask someone to read the Bible with you. Join in to welcome one refugee family as a church.

- Interactive idea: Interview a refugee live onstage during the service.

Week Three: Increasing Our Missional Intelligence (MQ) (chapters 5–8)

POINT ONE: Play to win—the goal of reaching all people groups (Matt. 24:14) (pp. **XX**?).

POINT TWO: Offer Jesus in a winsome way—the language of the kingdom of God (Mark 1:14–15; Matt. 13:24–46) (pages **XX**).

POINT THREE: Share good news so that it's good (pp. **XX**).

POINT FOUR: Practice a global role here—welcoming (Matt. 25:34–36), mobilizing (Num. 10:1–2), giving (Matt. 6:19–21), and praying (Eph. 6:10–20) (pages **XX**).

- Application for congregation: Come to a worship and prayer night for the nations. Give towards a selected work in an unreached people or place.
- Interactive idea: Tape butcher paper on all the walls with names of people groups. Ask congregation to write prayers on the walls during a reflective worship song.

Week Four: Going to the Nations (chapters 10–13)

POINT ONE: Should we GO until we're called to stay (Matt. 28:16–20 (pp. **XX**)?

POINT TWO: It takes surrender and perseverance (Matt. 16:24–26 (pp. **XX**)

POINT THREE: How to hear from God (John 16:13–15) (pp. **XX**).

- Application for congregation: Sign up for a short-term vision trip. Join a missional goer small group. Register for a Perspectives course.
- Interactive idea: Video chat live during the service with a field-worker living overseas in an unreached people group.

Utilize the following small group supplement plan:

- Launch an all-church, four-week small group series reading and discussing the book. Use the Small Group Plan divided into four sections, along with the Small Group Bible Reading List.

- Start additional six-month missional goer small groups, asking those with an interest in preparing to go to the nations to join. Set expectations for a higher level of participation and practice. Expect three hours of outreach time, three hours of time with God, and a three-hour group time per week. It's suggested to allow several weeks to discuss and practice one chapter of *Across the Street and Around the World* before moving on to the next chapter using the Small Group Plan along with the Small Group Reading Plan. Supplement with online resources found at [[insert URL]].

Small Group Plan

Gather a group of friends or your small group at church to read this book together, practicing it during the week and discussing it. Ask the group to read one chapter of the book during the week and come ready to discuss it during a regular meeting time. When you get together, read the Bible passage from the Small Group Bible Reading Plan to correspond with the *Across the Street and Around the World* chapter the group is reading that week, and use the following format each group time.

Review

1. What did you share with someone else about the book discussion or scripture last week? How did it go?
2. What did you do differently because of the book discussion or scripture last week? How did it go?
3. Discuss the "Reflection" questions at the end of the book chapter that the group read the previous week.

Discover

1. Read the scripture passage (see the Small Group Bible Reading Plan) for the chapter you're discussing out loud, twice.

2. Without looking at your Bibles, try to retell the passage out loud as a group. Someone can start, and the others will fill in what's missing. Have several people volunteer until the group has remembered the passage well. This will help you share the passage later.

3. As a group, make as many observations as possible. Focus on small and simple observations, not interpretations. "I noticed only two lepers came back to thank Jesus, instead of ten lepers" or "It looks like Jesus was traveling when it happened."

4. You could also ask:
   - What did you like about the scripture?
   - Did anything surprise you?
   - Did anything bother you?
   - What does this passage tell you about God?
   - What does this passage tell you about people?
   - What conclusions can we make about how the passage relates to our lives based on our discussion? *You could also ask:*
     —If this passage is true, how does it change how we see God?
     —If this passage is true, how does it change how we treat others?
     —If this passage is true, how does it change how we live?

Obey

1. Spend a few minutes in quiet, individual introspection, asking God how he wants you to put his words into practice. Write down an "I will . . ." statement to do in the next day or two to obey, practice, or internalize truth from the scripture. Discuss your answers.

Share

1. Do you know anyone who would benefit from hearing this story?

Connect

1. Does anyone have a celebration or a joy to share from the past week?
2. Does anyone have a challenge or struggle coming up this next week?
3. Is there any way the group can help with anyone's struggles this week?
4. Pray for each other in creative, structured ways, such as in pairs or by taking home the name of a person to pray for during the week.

Small Group Bible Reading List

Chapter 1: Adopting God's Heart for the Nations
- Read Genesis 12:1–3; Revelation 7:9–10.

Chapter 2: Interacting with Other Cultures Well
- Read 1 Corinthians 9:19–29.

Chapter 3: Engaging International Students and Welcoming Refugees
- Read Matthew 25:31–46.

Chapter 4: Cultivating Intentional Cross-Cultural Disciples
- Read 2 Timothy 2:2; 3:15–17.

Chapter 5: Offering Jesus in a Winsome Way to Other Cultures
- Read Mark 1:14–15; Matthew 13:24–46.

Chapter 6: Increasing your Missional Intelligence MQ
- Read Revelation 5:1–10; Matthew 24:14.

Chapter 7: Planning and Participating in Effective Short-Term Trips
- Read Luke 10:1–11.

Chapter 8: Mobilizing Inspirationally, Giving Extravagantly, and Praying Passionately
- Read Ephesians 6:10–20.

Chapter 9: Wrestling with Calling, Gifting, and Personalities

- Read Matthew 28:16–20.

Chapter 10: Dreaming about Professions and Earthly Impact

- Read Isaiah 61:1–6.

Chapter 11: Surrendering the American Dream

- Read Matthew 16:21–28.

  - Chapter 12: Getting Healthy and Hearing from GodRead John 10:1–16; 16:12–15.

Recommended Resources for Further Exploration

Chapter 3: Engaging International Students and Welcoming Refugees

On-Campus, Faith-Based International Student Organizations

- International Students Inc., www.isionline.org
- InterVarsity International Student Ministry, www.ism.intervarsity.org
- Navigators International Student Ministry, www.nav-ism.org

International Relief Agencies Helping Displaced Peoples

- The UN Refugee Agency (UNHCR), www.unhcr.org
- Care, www.care.org
- Doctors Without Borders, www.doctorswithoutborders.org

International Refugee Resettlement Organizations

- World Relief, www.worldrelief.org
- International Rescue Committee (IRC), www.rescue.org
- Lutheran Immigration Refugee Services, (LIRS) www.lirs.org
- Catholic Relief Services (CRS), www.crs.org

Chapter 4: Cultivating Intentional Cross-Cultural Disciples

Recommended Reading for Intentional Cross-Cultural Discipleship:

- *Contagious Disciple Making: Leading Others on a Journey of Discovery* (Nashville: Thomas Nelson, 2014) by David Watson and Paul Watson.
- *Spiritual Multiplication in the Real World: Why Some Disciple-Makers Reproduce When Others Fail* (n.p.: Multiplication Press, 2014) by Bob McNabb

Chapter 5: Offering Jesus in a Winsome Way to Other Cultures

Recommended Resources for Further Exploration:

- Kingdom of God: *Divine Conspiracy: Rediscovering Our Hidden Life in God* by Dallas Willard (New York: HarperCollins, 1998)
- Presenting only Jesus: *The Christ of the Indian Road* by E. Stanley Jones (Nashville: Abingdon, 1925)
- Creating bridges between faiths: *Muslims, Christians, and Jesus: Gaining Understanding and Building Relationships*, repr. ed., by Carl Medearis (Grand Rapids: Bethany House, 2008)
- Using honor language: *The 3D Gospel: Ministry in Guilt, Shame and Fear Cultures* by Jayson Georges (Timē Press, 2016)
- Speaking with kingdom language: www. thekingdomconversation.com

Chapter 6: Increasing Your Missional Intelligence (MQ)

International Sending Organizations:

- Ethnos360 (formerly New Tribes Mission, specializing in tribal animists and expanding now to all unreached people groups), https://ethnos360.org
- Frontiers (specializing in Muslims), www.frontiers.org
- International Mission Board (specializing in Hindus, Muslims, and Buddhists), https://imb.org
- OMF International (specializing in East Asian people groups), https://omf.org
- Wycliffe Bible Translators (specializing in Bible translation for unreached people groups) https://www.wycliff.org

Chapter 12: Getting Healthy and Hearing from God

Resources to Go Deeper in Getting Healthy and Hearing from God

- *A Guide for Listening and Inner Healing Prayer: Meeting God in the Broken Places* by Rusty Rustenbach (Carol Stream, IL: NavPress, 2011)
- *Experiencing God: Knowing and Doing the Will of God (Workbook)* by Henry Blackaby and Claude King (Nashville: Lifeway, 1990)
- *Hudson Taylor's Spiritual Secret* by Dr. and Mrs. Howard Taylor (Chicago: Moody, 2009)

Acknowledgments

To my field worker friends working in hard places who shall remain unnamed: You've mentored me, challenged me, and inspired me. Your stories and your path to the nations make this book genuine and true. Thank you for your perseverance, your willingness, and the suffering you choose to endure so that some from every nation will surrender to Jesus Christ, receive new life by the Spirit, and lavish worship on God.

David Shepherd and Rachel Boyle at DRS Agency, and Jessica Wong and the team at Thomas Nelson: Thank you for believing in the message of this book and taking a chance on a first-time author because of it. You are mobilizers in your area of giftedness and influence, for the nations!

Mike Ferrulli, Jayne Hamilton, Dave Keane, Luke Little, K. C. and Barb Rider, and Luke S., my hand-selected focus group of different backgrounds to help me gauge how readers might interact with the material: Thank you giving feedback, encouragement, and your unique impressions of the material, just when I needed it. I appreciate you.

Dr. Don Allen, Katie Whitehorn, and Jessica Wong: I am deeply indebted to your thorough, truthful, and brilliant insights and editing on every single page of this book. You influenced and shaped this book project in important and significant ways. And I am grateful for the many nights and weekends you gave to this project.

Emily, Jackson, Hayden, and Savannah: You contributed to this book too. As I wrote, I thought of all the things I'd like to say you—my disciples and children that I love so much. Stay close to Jesus, and he'll draw you to God's heart, to contribute to his purposes in your own unique way. Thank you for giving me time and space to write.

Paul: You have provided the stability, support, and encouragement for me to chase the dreams and passions God burns on my heart. Thank you for sending me on writing retreats, letting me stay up late nights (which resulted in late mornings), and giving me grace when my mind is distracted, preoccupied with yet another idea. You are good *for* me—and good *to* me.

Jesus: My friend, thank you for spending time with me while I wrote. You gave me constant wisdom, advice, and encouragement. Really, this is our book, because it's all about the adventures we've lived together.

About the Author

Jeannie Marie is a strategist for an international sending agency that recruits, trains, and sends long-term field-workers to more than fifty Muslim countries. An inspirational speaker and trainer, Jeannie also speaks around the country on how to create relational bridges with people from other cultures and faiths. She is on the board of directors for two nonprofits: Pathways to Global Understanding, a training course birthed from Perspectives; and Global Adventure Project, a group that places university students in strategic overseas internships.

Jeannie has extensive experience reaching out across the street to the nations in her neighborhood, and living around the world. She grew up as an expat in the Philippines, where her parents supported Bible translation for tribal groups. She worked in the corporate world, on staff for a local church, and in the community, welcoming international students and refugees in America, and also worked and lived in India. Jeannie and her husband and four children currently live in the suburbs of Phoenix, Arizona.

For more information, resources, and articles, or to book a speaking or training engagement, see www.jeannie-marie.com.

Notes

Chapter 1: Adopting God's Heart for the Nations

1. Story found in Matthew 25:31–40.

Chapter 2: Interacting with Other Cultures Well

1. Example based on cross-cultural internships, such as Launch Global (http://www.launchglobal.org/) and Training Ordinary Apprentices to Go (http://toag.org/).
2. Craig Storti, *Americans at Work: A Guide to the Can-Do People* (Boston: Intercultural Press, 2004), 13.
3. Sarah A. Lanier, *Foreign to Familiar: A Guide to Understanding Hot- and Cold-Climate Cultures* (Hagerstown, MD: McDougal, 2000).
4. Adapted from Central Christian Church in Mesa, Arizona, unpublished manual titled *Global Connection Trip Training*.
5. The Grove Bible Church, Chandler, AZ: (https://www.thegroveaz. org).

Chapter 3: Engaging International Students and Welcoming Refugees

1. Cite the Perspectives article in the book.
2. Data for SY (School Year) 2014–15 is from the Institute of International Education (IIE), "International Student Totals by Place of Origin, 2013/14–2014/15," Open Doors Report on International Educational Exchange (Washington, DC: IIE, 2015), http://www. migrationpolicy.org/article/international-students-united-states.

3. Ben Wolfgang, "Armed with U.S. Education, Many Leaders Take on World," *Washington Times*, August 19, 2012.

4. Information provided by International Students Inc., http://www. isionline.org/.

5. USA for UNHCR, "What Is a Refugee?" UNRefugees.org, accessed February 21, 2018, http://www.unrefugees.org/what-is-a-refugee/.

6. USA for UNHCR.

7. Care, "The Worse Refugee Crisis in History," Care.org, accessed February 21, 2018, http://www.care.org/emergencies/ global-refugee-crisis.

8. USA for UNHCR, "Refugees from These Three Countries Need the Hope YOU Provide," UNRefugees.org, accessed February 21, 2018, https://www.unrefugees.org/news/now-more-than-ever-refugees-from-these-three-countries-need-the-hope-usa-for-unhcr-donors-provide/.

9. Amnesty International, "Refugees Welcome Survey 2016—The Results," Amnesty.org, May 19, 2016, https://www.amnesty.org/en/ latest/news/2016/05/refugees-welcome-survey-results-2016/.

10. U.S. Department of State, U.S. Refugee Admissions Program FAQ, fact sheet, February 1, 2018, State.gov, https://www.state.gov/j/prm/ releases/factsheets/2018/277838.htm.

11. Susan Sperry, "The Current State of Refugee Resettlement in the U.S.," June 8, 2017. http://www.ucc.org/ justice_immigration_worship_biblical-references-to.

12. USA for UNHCR, "Information on UNHCR Resettlement," UNRefugees.org, accessed February 21, 2018, http://www.unhcr.org/ en-us/information-on-unhcr-resettlement.html.

13. "United Church of Christ, Biblical References to Immigrants and Refugees," UCC.org, accessed February 21, 2018, http://www.ucc.org/ justice_immigration_worship_biblical-references-to.

14. U.S. Department of State, U.S. Refugee Admissions Program FAQ.

15. Sperry, "The Current State of Refugee Resettlement in the U.S."

16. To learn more about helping people recover from trauma, read Judith Herman, MD, *Trauma and Recovery: The Aftermath of Violence—From Domestic Abuse to Political Terror*, with a new epilogue by the author. (New York: Basic Books, 2015).

17. SOURCE NEEDED.

Chapter 4: Cultivating Intentional Cross-Cultural Disciples

1. The discovery approach outlined in this section isn't new but has been championed in recent times by David Watson and articulated well in David Watson and Paul Watson's *Contagious Disciple Making: Leading Others on a Journey of Discovery* (Nashville: Thomas Nelson, 2014).

2. The idea of using 2 Timothy 2:2 to train believers to read the Bible with others came from Bob McNabb and is articulated in his excellent discipleship book, *Spiritual Multiplication in the Real World: Why Some Disciple-Makers Reproduce When Others Fail* (n.p.: Multiplication Press, 2014).

3. All tips are adapted from InterVarsity International training videos. See "International Student Ministry Students," InterVarsity, accessed February 22, 2018, https://ism.intervarsity.org/student-leaders.

4. You can find a list of Discovery Bible Study passages at https://internationalproject.org/ or by reading anything by David Watson, who popularized the Discovery approach.

5. Jerry Trousdale, *Miraculous Movements: How Hundreds of Thousands of Muslims Are Falling in Love with Jesus* (Nashville: Thomas Nelson, 2012).

Chapter 5: Offering Jesus in a Winsome Way to Other Cultures

1. E. Stanley Jones, *The Christ of the Indian Road* (1925; Nashville: Abingdon, 2014).

2. The book of Matthew, written to a Jewish audience, used the words "Kingdom of Heaven' instead of "kingdom of God" perhaps because Jews avoided using the sacred name of God if at all possible. See Matt. 3:2; 4:17; 5:3, 10, among others.

3. Trousdale, *Miraculous Movements*, 191 (see chap. 1, n. 3).

Chapter 6: Increasing Your Missional Intelligence (MQ)

1. Martin Luther King Jr. *Strength to Love*, repr. (Fortress Press, 1977), 46.
2. Visit http://www.perspectives.org/ for more information.
3. Visit http://www.perspectives.org/ for more information.
4. From the 1982 Lausanne Committee Chicago meeting. See "What Is a People Group?" JoshuaProject.net, https://joshuaproject.net/resources/articles/what_is_a_people_group.
5. Frank Newport, "Percentage of Christians in U.S. Drifting Down, but Still High," Gallup, December 24, 2015, http://www.gallup.com/poll/187955/percentage-christians-drifting-down-high.aspx.
6. M. David Sills, *The Missionary Call: Find Your Place in God's Plan for the World* (Chicago: Moody, 2008), 182.
7. "Coca-Cola's Growth Potential & Market Share" SureDividend.com, updated January 14, 2017, by the *Financial Canadian*, http://www.suredividend.com/coca-colas-growth-potential/
8. J. Dudley Woodberry, ed., *From Seed to Fruit: Global Trends, Fruitful Practices, and Emerging Trends Among Muslims* (Pasadena: William Carey Library, 2011).
9. Ralph D. Winter and Bruce A. Koch, "Finishing the Task: The Unreached Peoples Challenge," in *Perspective on the World Christian Movement: A Reader Fourth*, 4th ed., ed. Ralph D. Winter and Stephen C. Hawthorne (Pasadena: William Carey Library, 2009), 540.
10. The Traveling Team, "Missions Stats: The Current State of the World," TheTravelingTeam.com, last updated April 2017 from Operation World and Joshua Project, http://www.thetravelingteam.org/stats/.
11. Data provided by Regional Strategy Coordinators at Frontiers USA, https://www.frontiersusa.org/.
12. The Traveling Team, "Missions Stats."
13. Winter and Koch, "Finishing the Task," 545.
14. The Traveling Team, "Missions Stats."
15. The Traveling Team.

Chapter 7: Planning and Participating in Effective Short-Term Trips

1. Steve Corbett and Brian Fikkert with Katie Casselberry, *Helping Without Hurting in Short-Term Missions* (Chicago: Moody, 2014).
2. Steve Corbett and Brian Fikkert, *When Helping Hurts: How to Alleviate Poverty Without Hurting the Poor . . . and Yourself* (Chicago: Moody, 2014), 101.

Chapter 8: Mobilizing Inspirationally, Giving Extravagantly, and Praying Passionately

1. Steve Shadrach "Mobilization: The Key to World Evangelization," The Traveling Team, accessed February 23, 2018, http://www.thetravelingteam.org/articles/mobilization.
2. Randy Alcorn, *The Treasure Principle: Unlocking the Secret of Joyful Giving* (Colorado Springs: Multnomah, 2001), 18.
3. Alcorn, *The Treasure Principle*, 40.
4. The Traveling Team, "Missions Stats: The Current State of the World" (see chap. 6, n. 10).
5. Daniel Waheli, *Lessons Learned in the Lion's Den: Imprisoned for Sharing Jesus*, (Pasadena: William Carey Library, 2014).
6. Dr. and Mrs. Howard Taylor, *Hudson Taylor's Spiritual Secret* (Chicago: Moody, 1989, 2009).
7. Trousdale, *Miraculous Movements*, 54 (see chap. 4, n. 3).
8. Richard Foster, *Celebration of Discipline: The Path to Spiritual Growth* (San Fransisco: HarperOne, 1998), 33, 34.
9. Jason Mandryk, *Operation World: The Definitive Prayer Guide to Every Nation*, 7th ed. (Downers Grove, IL: IVP, 2010).

Chapter 9: Wrestling with Calling, Gifting, and Personalities

1. Popular language learning methods among field-workers include the Growing Participator Approach (GPA) and the Language Acquisition Made Practical (Lamp) program.
2. "Mother Teresa Quotes," BrainyQuote.com, accessed February

23, 2018, https://www.brainyquote.com/quotes/quotes/m/
mothertere158109.html.

3. Watson and Watson, *Contagious Disciple Making*, xi–xiv (see chap. 4, n. 1).

4. Walt Unsworth, *Everest: A Mountaineering History*, 3rd ed. (Seattle: Mountaineers, 2000), 236.

5. Ken Curtis, PhD, "Whatever Happened to the Twelve Apostles?" Christianity.com, April 28, 2010, http://www.christianity.com/ church/church-history/timeline/1–300/whatever-happened-to-the- twelve-apostles-11629558.html.

Chapter 10: Dreaming About Overseas Professions and Earthly Impact

1. BAM and B4T are networks of believers starting profitable businesses in foreign countries to disciple people into faith in Jesus Christ.

2. Examples of discipleship tools used in church planting are Discovery Bible Studies (DBS), Training for Trainers (T4T), and the Building on Firm Foundations Chronological Bible Study.

3. David Garrison, *Church Planting Movements: How God Is Redeeming a Lost World*, 5th ed. (Bangalore: Wigtake Resources, 2006), 27.

4. Corbett and Fikkert, *When Helping Hurts*, 99 (see chap. 7, n. 2).

5. Corbett and Fikkert, 99–101.

6. See the Global CHE Network website at https://www.chenetwork. org/.

7. United Nations, "World Day of Social Injustice: 20 February," UN.org, accessed February 23, 2018, http://www.un.org/en/events/ socialjusticeday/.

8. United Nations, *United Nations Literacy Decade: Education for All; International Plan of Action; Implementation of General Assembly Resolution 56/116. Report of the Secretary General* (New York: United Nations, 2002).

9. Central Intelligence Agency, "The World Fact Book," CIA.gov, accessed February 23, 2018, https://www.cia.gov/library/publications/ the-world-factbook/fields/2103.html.

Chapter 12: Getting Healthy and Hearing from God

1. Rusty Rustenbach, *A Guide for Listening and Inner Healing Prayer: Meeting God in the Broken Places* (Colorado Springs: NavPress, 2011), 35.

2. Henry and Richard Blackaby and Claude King, *Experiencing God: Knowing and Doing the Will of God* (Nashville: B&H, 2008) 9–10.

3. Soren Kierkegaard, *Christian Discourses*, trans. Walter Lowrie (New York: Oxford University Press, 1940).

4. Dr. and Mrs. Howard Taylor, *Hudson Taylor's Spiritual Secret* (Chicago: Moody Publishers, 1989, 2009).

CPSIA information can be obtained
at www.ICGtesting.com
Printed in the USA
LVOW03s1908200418
574346LV00001B/3/P